Richard Henderson

The Jealousy of Jonah

A Christian devotional commentary on
The Book of Jonah as translated in
the Authorised (King James) Version of the Bible

the columba press

First published in 2006 by
the columba press
55A Spruce Avenue, Stillorgan Industrial Park,
Blackrock, Co Dublin

Cover by Bill Bolger
The cover image is from a stained-glass window at St Fin Barre's Cathedral, Cork. Jonah and the Story of the Gourd. Designed by William Burges, 1869 and made by Saunders & Co, 1878.
Photography by David Lawrence. Copyright by The Representative Church Body of the Church of Ireland. Reproduced by permission of the Cathedral Select Vestry and the Respresentative Church Body.
Origination by The Columba Press
Printed in Ireland by ColourBooks Ltd, Dublin

ISBN 1 85607 522 2

Table of Contents

Acknowledgements

I am grateful to many friends for reading over various drafts of the manuscript and for their critical comments. In particular, I should like to thank Dr Eamonn Conway, Fr Patrick Walsh, Dr Margaret Daly-Denton, Henry Noltie, Patrick Rolleston, Michael Burrows, and especially my mother Susan Henderson who provided the illustrations.

The Book of Jonah has been so much part of my thinking and speaking for so long, I may have inadvertently quoted from sources without proper acknowledgement – to such as these I apologise and at the same time say, 'thank you'.

I am very thankful to the Church of Ireland for letting me have a Sabbatical for three months in 2004, when the first draft of the text was written.

Most of all I thank my wife Anita and children Cicely, Pippa and Jack for their patient indulgence and constant love and support.

Richard Henderson
June 2005

A Note on Abbreviations
Biblical references to the Book of Jonah are given simply by their Chapter and Verse; e.g. Jonah 1:8 is given as (1:8)
Other books of the Bible are given by their standard abbreviations:
Mt = Gospel of Matthew
Mk = Gospel of Mark
Lk = Gospel of Luke
Jn = Gospel of John... *NB not to be confused with Jonah (Jon)*
Gen = Genesis
Ex = Exodus
Isa = Isaiah
Ps = Psalms
Prov = Proverbs

Author's Preface

I first became interested in the priceless Book of Jonah – which I consider to be one the most important (and Christian) in the Old Testament – by accident. As part of a series for clergy on the Minor Prophets, I was to give a talk on Haggai, until a telephone call came from the Jonah speaker saying he had the 'flu' and would I swap? I shall always be grateful for this unexpected change.

Like most people, including a Dublin Taxi driver I met recently, all I knew about the book was the whale. I also had in my mind a few Sunday School images, in bright primary colours on thick board, of a daft little prophet with a stick and a big happy whale. Further, I was vaguely aware of people who were anxious to prove that a person could survive three days and nights in a whale, but I felt that silly discussions of this sort succeeded only in making God's miraculous work unstable and quirky. It seemed obvious that to insist on its miraculous nature was to lose its miraculous meaning.

I Iardly enough to give a talk to anyone; worse still, to clergy.

But what *did* it mean? I read it a couple of times (it has the great virtue of being short – only four very short chapters[1]) and could not grasp any meaning at all. It was either a quaint little story to arouse brief amusement before passing on to more serious stuff, or there was a need to dig deeper, much deeper. I had no helpful commentaries on it, and began to panic because of my deadline. So I went to visit the local Roman Catholic priest

1. As Father Mapple says in *Moby Dick*, 'Shipmates, this book , containing only four chapters – four yarns – is one of the smallest strands in the mighty cable of the scriptures ...'

who said, 'Ah God, Richard, now you're asking' but he eventually dug out an old copy of the *Jerome Biblical Commentary*. An article in there[2] began to open my eyes, and the scales have been falling off ever since; I must have read Jonah a hundred times[3] and always have seen new things.

I hope this may be true for my readers, too.

✠ *Richard Tuam:*

2. Jean C. McGowan RSCJ, Chapter 39 *The Jerome Biblical Commentary*, 1968

3. I am not alone in this: C. H. Cornhill is quoted in *The Interpreter's Bible* (p 875) as saying the same and adding, 'this book is one of the deepest and grandest ever written ... take off your shoes, for the ground whereon thou standest is holy ground'.

Introduction

The little Book of Jonah is a pearl of the greatest price. It is truly a narrative for today that seems to touch and redeem all the nerves of our current condition, and make sense of the bewildering conflicts of a violent and beautiful world. Psychologically aware, accurate, compassionate, humorous and hopeful, the book is dynamite; I am half surprised that it has been sitting so meekly on my bookshelves without explosively making its presence known.

In its few short pages, the book touches all the personal things that matter most to all of us – life and death, love and hate, forgiveness and retribution, belonging and separation, gain and loss, hope and despair. The religious believer also finds that the author, with a marvellous sureness and subtlety, plucks and harmonises all the strings of religious life: repentance and faith, vocation and ministry, grace and judgement, sin and salvation, forgiveness and reconciliation – even predestination and free will. None of these is sold cheap; rather, they are seen as part of the most necessary and beautiful picture of a divine and universal purpose to lose nothing that has been made.

In broader terms, it can become for Christians a parable of the church – or at least the role of the believer in an unbelieving world. In a gentle and humorous way, it is the most powerful commentary on sectarianism – where religion and national identity can combine to make people lethally uncaring and ignorant of others. As such, it is one of the few books in the bible to offer a realistic criticism of the wrong sort of religious zeal. There are many other implications for the contemporary church as it struggles with disappointment, low numbers and loss of face – and as it anxiously works to identify its continuing mission and ministry when so much has been stripped from it. The text of Jonah is written after such crisis, and raises the question of how those who possess the historic faith should operate in vastly changed circumstances. In such circumstances, the choice is between ever-narrowing introversion, and catching a wonderful vision of something new, far greater than anything perceived before; between nurturing the wounds of history and entering the uncharted ground of liberating forgiveness. From a pastoral and psychological point of view, it is a book that suggests the best ways of opening up this great vision, dealing all the while with reluctance, even intransigence and bigotry.

Broader still, in a world of atrocities that are often undergirded by religious zeal or deeply flawed high moral ground, it is a book about risk; letting go the familiar footholds, and taking a sacrificial plunge into uncertainty when the storm threatens to engulf us all. Risk for Jonah is forced upon him, but the invitation for the reader is to take the risk voluntarily.

Yet everything is always under the umbrella of a God with limitless love who shows us our need to change. In doing this, the book also hints at *how* to change the sort of intense religious zeal and prejudice that makes for shocking indifference to the rights, feelings and opportunities of others. It is deeply human, and totally divine. It leads us through loss and uncertainty into the ways everlasting.

I need to add some important comments at this stage. Jonah is in the *Old* Testament, yet I have said that book of Jonah is deeply Christian. I mean by this that it is so full of allusions to the deepest and most sublime virtues that are to be found in the life, death and teaching of Jesus Christ. Moreover, it was clearly influential in the way Jesus viewed his own ministry and teaching; indeed Jonah was reputed to be buried very near to where Jesus grew up, making him their 'local man'. Thus, although it is 'against the rules', I believe it is right and essential to link the allusions of Jonah with the rest of scripture, including the New Testament. The book is indeed prophecy, not in the sense of a mere prediction of the future, but in that it unerringly speaks of truths that stand for all time, and are supremely embodied and demonstrated in Christ.

I also need to say something about the style of this book. I am not a biblical scholar, and do not wish to pretend to be. I have chosen the King James Version of the bible because its slightly remote language constantly encourages the reader to see the poetic meaning of the text. My main interest has been in the power of the story as told, and as it strikes me, as just one reader. Given the popular perception of Jonah as a quirky children's story, I have sought to open up the text just enough to suggest, but not prescribe, its poetic resonance.

I have not wanted to obscure too much the narrative thrust of the text; it can be read as the text itself (in **Bold** type), as the running commentary that follows each verse, and also (at the risk of irritating my readers) at a third level – the footnotes and boxes. The footnotes serve two functions: there are of course the usual cross references, but I have also occasionally used them, and the boxes, to indicate some of the pleasant digressions suggested so powerfully by the narrative.

Through it all, in narrative, commentary, footnotes, and boxes, I have been wanting to ask what this little book might mean to our contemporary world.

Jonah – A Few Critical Considerations

This is hardly a scholarly analysis, but to get to the root of the special relevance of Jonah, it is a great help to think for a moment about when, where and why it was written. At the same time, to get totally submerged in some of the scholarly discussions can make one lose the narrative thrust, economy and elegance of the text. My chief aim in this book, as I have said, is to treat the story as narrative and to offer devotional and reflective comment. What I am about to argue is evidenced chiefly from the text itself, so examples and corroboration are included where relevant in the commentary and not here.

The first and obvious question for twenty-first century minds may be: 'Is it historical?' By this I mean to ask whether it is a strictly factual account of what actually happened. There are very many good reasons for thinking that it is not.

Firstly, the places and timing of events are only mentioned when they have a *religious* meaning; nothing, nobody and nowhere is incidental to the story. Places such as Nineveh and Tarshish and even the name of the prophet – Jonah – are pregnant with association and meaning.

Secondly, the bizarre elements such as the great fish, the gourd that grows and dies in a day, the cattle wandering about in sackcloth, the repentance (with no dissenters!) of a whole city, are hardly likely in the normal course of things. You can perhaps try to believe them literally if you wish, but it does not help the story – and possibly hinders it.[4] Of course, God *could* provide for

4. As very many have tried to do, (e.g. Calvin, Pusey) but, as F. R. Horton comments, 'it is humiliating for a commentator to collect doubtful stories of sailors swallowed by sharks and vomited out alive'.

these things but the danger is that treating this as a simple miracle story means that one can simply say 'How remarkable!' (or 'How miraculous!') and pass on, unchanged, except by momentary wonder. If we do *not* regard it as the one story in the one place and time, we cannot easily dismiss it – thus it remains our story and a story for every place and time. The same is true for the whole bible, if only we could see it. Regarding the fish, the ancient world abounded with legends of great fish. Thus, as we shall see, the whole genius and thrust of the book is the conflation of all sorts of familiar strands within Jewish religion and beyond. So the bizarre is incorporated to show a meaning, or teach a lesson, maybe even to make us smile – but not to describe an event. In this book, the miracles show God's purpose and mercy more than giving demonstrations of God's power and might.

Thirdly, it does not read like the histories to be found in other parts of the bible. It ends abruptly, leaving *religious* questions in the reader's mind. There is no tidying up; no details such as 'Jonah lived to be a hundred and ninety years old and is buried with his ancestors in Galilee'; no story of what happened next to Nineveh and so on. Even the name of the Ninevite king is not given – quite unlike the chronicles elsewhere in scripture. Rather, the story has the skill, finesse and economy of a finely delineated painting or novel. History, as it actually happens, is more ragged. By contrast, this whole story builds up to a pointed question, and as you close the book you are left asking, 'how would it be if ...? 'what if ...?' 'suppose it could ...?'

One might add a few extra points that throw doubt over the strict historicity of the book. Nineveh is portrayed as being very big indeed – taking three days to cross.[5] That is *very* big, and no archaeological evidence exists for this, neither for the sort of total religious transformation that is described in the story. Some have said that 'greater Nineveh' could, like 'Greater

5. Even on foot, this is a long way. The *spiritual* significance of the three days is a much more interesting line of enquiry – see comments on 1:17 and 3:3.

London', indicate a whole district, but again to push this literalism seems unnecessary.[6]

Furthermore, the Jews firmly positioned the Book of Jonah among the prophets, and not the histories. Christ himself, who placed such emphasis on this wonderful book, refers to the sign (a pointer, not a destination) of the *prophet* Jonah.[7] In fact, the book is not a book of prophecies such as you might find, for example, in Isaiah; there are no oracles, detailed judgements or hopes. Where there are the familiar impassioned pleas of the prophets, they are most significantly said by God and directed to Jonah. By contrast, Jonah's prophecy of eight words is short indeed: 'Yet forty days and Nineveh shall be overthrown' (3:4). But we should note this: although the Book of Jonah is not really a book of prophecies (or a history book), it is most definitely a history of *what it is like* to be a prophet. Here, the relationship of God to the prophet and the prophet to God are intimately if ironically portrayed.[8]

The above is supported by giving some thought to the literary form of the book. It looks very like a parable: the message comes first – and the familiar details, people, and places are brought in to illustrate the message. It is full of deliberate irony (e.g. the contrasting stories of Elijah and Jonah): history is indeed ironic sometimes, but not with any consistency. The book ends, as we have seen, with a question. A parable is a story that invites us to lay our own life story alongside the one we have heard; to use the dreadful language of school examinations, 'compare and contrast'. If you look at some of the parables of Jesus, you find exactly the same pattern – for example the Good

6. Calvin, in his commentary, places elaborate emphasis on the population count of 120,000 (see 4:11), and suggests that this was the total head count only of the innocent – i.e. young children. He further suggests that the three days' journey is justified on the grounds that this is how long it might take to proclaim the message in all the streets and squares.
7. Mt 12:38-42; Lk 11: 29-32
8. For a short discussion on this, see Ceresko, A. R., *Jonah*, quoting von Rad 'Prophetic proclivity for self-questioning is one of the best aspects of its spirit'.

Samaritan.[9] Did a man really walk on the notorious Jerusalem to Jericho road, did it really happen as history – or was it local detail and to bring the point home? Note, too, that the parable also ends with a question, 'Which of these do you think was neighbour?' A parable is a story to inspire, rebuke, correct, parody, above all reveal what you understand – and need yet to understand. If a question is posed at the end, it is to set you thinking and to leave you thinking. Jonah has just this literary power.

Still with literary form, consider what is called 'Clip Art' on your computer. You can access all sorts of visual images from a huge collection, and place them where you want in the text you are writing. They are recognisable, and preformed, but you can place them in new places – to see how they look, or to make, illustrate, even to qualify a point. The Book of Jonah is completely full of this technique, as we shall see. There are no drawings, of course, but I shall still refer to them as Clip Art. They are quotes, or near-quotes[10] from the scriptures, that would have been so familiar to the first readers; the skill is to introduce ancient, universal, recognisable and accepted truths into new places. This is a most powerful device and is used with consummate skill by the author of Jonah. We Christians have had it drummed into us that 'a text without a context is a pretext'. Fair enough, but the art of Jonah is to take a text into a new context; this is surely what the best preaching is about.[11]

Before leaving literary form, we should note that there is a very great body of literature on the extraordinarily careful structure and composition of the narrative. It seems hardly relevant for this commentary, but is exhaustively discussed by Sasson.[12] In passing we might note that genuine historians do not occupy themselves with perfect symmetry and linguistic form in their factual accounts of the past.

9. Lk 10:25-37.

10. We should note that the Clip Art is not always *verbatim*, but its provenance is very clear.

11. Asking, 'how does ancient truth still apply?'

12. Jack M. Sasson, *Jonah*. See especially Introduction, but also verse by verse commentary.

This leads to a further question that is to do with the date of the book. Considering this question is the most fruitful of all to understanding the motivation behind the composition of the story and its astonishing relevance for today. On the face of it, it seems to be a book by (or about) the prophet of the same name referred to in the second book of Kings (2 Kings 14:25). That historical Jonah, son of Amittai, was adjutant to a successful king in the eighth century BC – expanding his territory, and imagining that this extension of power indicated God's approval and endorsement. However, much of the language of the book is not from the eighth century; many of its words are only found in later Hebrew literature.[13] So we have to pause for thought. Such 'later' words could have been added later on, but it does not read like a clumsily or anachronistically edited text. Let me put it simply and crudely: if you found lots of twentieth-century words like 'OK' and 'Coca Cola' in a work supposed to be by Shakespeare, you would disregard them, or else you would conclude that the whole work was written much later and not by Shakespeare.

Further, and most importantly, the text reveals a real interest in evaluating the relation of Israel to other nations in the Gentile world, reminiscent especially of the book of Ruth, but also Ezra and Nehemiah. All these were written after the Exile and humiliation of the Jewish nation. This is the sort of interest you would not expect to find when fortunes were ascendant (as in the eighth century before Christ). It resonates much better with a people who have suffered some awful catastrophe and are forced by this circumstance to see things afresh, and to bring into their thinking concerns and responsibilities that had been avoided or unnecessary before. What do religious post-Holocaust people think? What can they think? To take just one example, how do Rwandan Christians interpret the horrors of their genocide? What does it say about God, and about religion and about tribalism and indeed all humanity?

So the Book of Jonah begins to gain especial relevance to a

13. See, for example, Mc Gowan, Horton and others.

broken 'church' or religious community that can no longer cling to assumed decency or former authority and power.[14] It also speaks to any nation whose sense of destiny and moral virtue has overstepped its proper boundaries, even if it has been in response to being overrun by the undeniable wickedness or godless actions of others.[15] In fact it speaks very directly to any 'post' society when traditional belief and value has been thrown into crisis or led to things that are, in turn, manifestly shameful. New questions are forced about God's nature and purpose, even existence. The option is either to lapse into indifference, defensiveness and denial (where 'otherness' is to be ignored, ostracised, fought, destroyed, and where there is no criticism of self[16]) – or to address these questions and, willingly or unwillingly, to embrace the crisis this precipitates, often at further, almost unbearable, personal cost (as we shall see when the story of Jonah unfolds). The choice is between a pathetic and narrow particularism that energetically reinforces the familiar despite all the evidence outside, or courageous risk and honesty that discovers, through loss, a wonderful liberty and generous new vision of God.

If these surmises are correct, then we may put it bluntly. Jonah is a pious but narrow-minded nationalist, unable to come to terms with decline rather than growth, loss rather than victory, captivity rather than new-found freedom. He represents a more-or-less defensive minority, finding consolation but not much transformation in his religion. He remains psychologically the eighth century victorious prophet, but *transported* by the story into a vastly changed world – and the question asked of him is: 'How would you fare now?'

The long and short of this is that most scholars believe the work to be 'post-Exilic', probably dating from 400-200 BC. For

14. For a contemporary example, one might consider post-Ascendancy culture in the Church of Ireland.
15. This has been a strongly and widely held view of the American response post '9-11'.
16. This is the most odious preoccupation of the modern tabloids, and much religious thinking.

myself, it is the most inspired parable of imagination, a midrash founded on all sorts of historic and theological pieces, cut and pasted into a narrative for that pre-Christian world, and for the many post-Christian worlds where history is so sadly repeated. It is for this reason endlessly contemporary in a world that continues to change, and especially to us in modern times when change is everywhere.

Jonah – Chapter One

1. Now the word of the LORD came unto Jonah the son of Amittai, saying ...

We can imagine Jonah, carefully and quietly pursuing his religious duties, making the best of things, but sighing from time to time. Occasionally he bemoans the changed fate of his people, and sometimes he is downright angry at the wickedness of Nineveh, muttering that they should not be allowed to get away with it. But he is content enough in his cocooned little world of orthodoxy.

Then the *word* comes and nothing can ever be the same again for him.[17] The formula 'the word of the LORD came' is the indication of divine calling, applied to very many other biblical prophets.[18] The Word *is*. Not just *words*, but the creative word, disturbing, transforming and saving, always attaining its end; the word of God goes out and always (even by the most devious routes of what we call 'free will', as we shall see) achieves its purpose.[19]

When the Word comes to Jonah, it does not just instruct him, it *enlists* him. Vocation is God's initiative, God's choice, God's purpose, God's instrument, even God's witness. Vocation and election are not for our amusement or edification, still less our pride, but primarily for God's purpose. Once the word has come, Jonah has to move – the reluctant conscript. Jonah now has a faith *and* a vocation, and the combination is not welcome;

17. The word had only to come to Jonah for his situation to be genuinely and totally changed even though he himself was not changed. Ellul p 23.
18. See, for example, Gen 15, 2 Sam 24:11, 1 Kings 6:11ff, Ezek1:3 etc.
19. Isa 55:11, 45:23.

suddenly infinitely more is demanded of him. Once he is called in this way, whether in disobedience or reluctant obedience, he cannot help but be as salt in the world – an agent of saving transformation; hardest of all, he has to be transformed himself, even lost, in the process. As with many other prophets, each has his own excuse,[20] but each eventually says 'send me'. It just takes a good bit longer in the case of Jonah (3:1).

The fact of the word *coming* is important also: God is involved – with Jonah, with Nineveh (1:2, 3:2), and ultimately concerned for the whole world (4:11). The power of the Word coming is at the centre of all scripture, and for Christians is most profoundly seen when the word comes to Mary and dwells there by consent – this is our salvation. Indeed the Book of Jonah itself is a book about salvation (see 2:9), but for all its developed breadth and complexity it is initiated by the simply stated 'coming of the word'.

For Jonah, the coming of the word is profoundly disturbing and many with vocations can testify to this. Psalm 139, frequently alluded to in the text, has these lines:

> 'You hem me in, behind and before. You have laid your hand upon me'. Ps 139:5

The hand on the shoulder is not always a comfortable awareness: is it the support of a friend – or might it be the arresting and binding hand of the law – caught at last? Certainly it is not comfortable for Jonah who remains disturbed in every sense increasingly throughout the book, but it all begins here when, as P. G. Wodehouse would say, 'he was knocked off his perch'.

Why should God disturb him thus? We may deduce from the emerging story that Jonah's orthodoxy and piety contain the right truth but encapsulated in the wrong place; he has been like a seed in a packet, far from the alien soil that is the only place for it to grow.

We should say a little about the person and name of 'Jonah'. The eighth century Jonah was from Gath Hepher in Zebulon, on

20. See for example Ex 4:1, Isa 6:5, Jer 1:6.

the highway of the Gentiles with much news coming from Nineveh, and he reputedly died not far from where Jesus was later to grow up. The name means 'dove' and has connotations of a silly innocence.[21] This sets the scene for the way in which God deals with Jonah – he is viewed with knowledge combined with affection – the essential combination for constructive and healing criticism.

2. Arise, go to Nineveh, that great city, and cry against it; *Arise* is the disturbing instruction that Jonah has to obey; he has no option to stay put, whether he obeys with ready feet or whether he demurs. But the destination is appalling – Nineveh. It is like telling a turkey to vote for Christmas. Nineveh was the notorious epicentre of one of the most military, cruel and 'god-less' people of antiquity. As such, they were both human and spiritual enemies to the Jews and symbolic of man's omnipotence and pride at the height of their power. Nineveh was also a long way away, some 750 miles, and Jonah was asked to go *alone* to a city of 120,000 people. Jonah is asked to walk into the lions' den. He is asked to go into the depths of darkness and strike a solitary light, sacrificing his status, wealth, repose, security and very possibly his life in the meanwhile. These things would be deterrent enough, and we might for like reason question and avoid our calling. To the Jewish reader, these would be very good reasons for querying whether this was a *bona fide* calling from God. But with the most ingenious twist they do not explain why Jonah refuses to go (we have to wait for Chapter 4 to see the true reason). **... for their wickedness is come up before me.** God indicates that he is familiar with the wickedness of Nineveh, and is thus totally aware of the people Jonah despises. The phraseology is Clip Art from the story of Sodom and Gomorrah where likewise the wickedness comes before God.[22] So, as the word of the Lord comes (as it were) *down* to Jonah, the sins of Nineveh

21. In Hosea 7:11 Ephraim is seen as a silly dove. Jerome comments that the root of 'Jonah' may be from the Hebrew word *Yanah,* with the significance of *dolens*, complaining. This is apt also.
22. Gen 13:13.

have come *up* to God. Both directions indicated very surely that God is intimately involved with his creation, and the response from the hero of the book is to go sideways.

3. But Jonah rose up to flee unto Tarshish ...
The delightful cat and mouse game now begins, but we should pause on the word 'But'. Throughout the book (1:3, 1:4, 1:17, 4:1, 4:7), there is a constant dialogue between Jonah and God, often with action and counteraction, as in a chess game. This is the first 'but' in the King James translation – a counter *move* because Jonah has no power directly to counter*mand* the Grandmaster. Jonah did indeed arise, as commanded, but he rose up to flee, and to flee to Tarshish. Tarshish is generally recognised to be Greek city Tartessos, a Phoenician colony in Southern Spain. This was at the far end of the Mediterranean, and as such the farthest perceived boundary of the world. So it is as if God said, 'Arise and go into the lions' den', and Jonah replied, 'I'll arise all right, but I'm off to Timbuktu.'

... from the presence of the Lord ... Here is the first irony, repeated later in this verse. There are repeated echoes of Psalm 139 which affirms:

> If I ascend up into heaven, thou art there: if I make my bed in hell, behold, thou art there.
> If I take the wings of the morning, and dwell in the uttermost parts of the sea;
> Even there shall thy hand lead me, and thy right hand shall hold me. *Ps139:8-10*

So Jonah's neurotic running away is illogical – he cannot possibly flee *from the presence of the Lord*. Moreover he runs against, for the first but by no means the last time, the very faith he professes. It would be quite untenable for a Jew at this stage of history, familiar with the Psalm above and also:

> Holy, holy, holy, is the Lord of hosts: the whole earth is full of his glory. *Isa 6:3*

If Jonah thinks that by a little bit of geographical separation, he is breaking the power of his vocation and election, it is a subtle indicator of his narrow view of God's presence. He believes, like his eighth century antecedent, that the presence and favour of God is limited to *believers'* territory, and indicated by it. There are many religious who unknowingly assume or actually believe that today. Nonetheless, this childish faith, combined with acute awareness and concern for the things of God, begins to arouse in the reader's mind an affectionate sympathy for the terrified prophet. There are echoes, too, of Adam and Eve naïvely hiding in the bushes from God:

> And they heard the voice of the Lord God walking in the garden in the cool of the day: and Adam and his wife hid themselves from the presence of the Lord God amongst the trees of the garden. *Gen 3:8*

... and went down to Joppa ...

Joppa is Jaffa, a large port where Jonah can be sure of two things – anonymity, and the chance to get on a ship bound for distant shores. He is marvellously described in Hermann Melville's *Moby Dick* as skulking around the wharves, having already descended into a totally alien culture, moving among people he has never met, and never even considered. The place brims with pagan seafarers, Gentiles all. The strange people, sights and smells are welcome because Jonah is getting away from it all.

The psychology of his flight and attitude are perfectly summarised by the Irish expression – he was going 'out foreign'.

and he found a ship going to Tarshish ...

So Jonah has found his ship that he fancies is going to the ends of the earth. When he boards it, he spontaneously creates a new and very uneasy fellow-ship, with fascinating religious 'chemistry'; a single believer in a ship of pagans. We shall say more about the ship later, but we should note two more things in this verse.

so he paid the fare thereof ...

I am told that the language does not imply that he just paid his personal fare like and decent law-abiding citizen. Rather, he paid the fare of the *whole* ship, chartered it. This is a delightful humorous touch, slightly reminiscent of people who buy an extra seat on a plane for their Stradivari 'cello. So desperate is his flight that he says, 'Forget the cabin fare, I'll take the whole ship, so long as we leave now.'

and went down into it ... from the presence of the Lord

His descent continues; Jonah has been told to get *up* and go east. Jonah has gone *down* and gone west. He goes down to Joppa, down into the ship, down into the sides of the ship, down into the sea, down into the fish, down to the roots of the mountains, before being vomited up where he started.[23] Psychologically and spiritually he has gone down in a far more significant way, as we shall see in Chapters 2 and 4.

4. But the Lord ...

Here is the second 'but' as already observed. There is great power in the equivalent words 'but God', frequently used in the New Testament when an insoluble or intractable problem has been posed. There is no answer until 'but God' and therein is the whole answer – God's person and nature, power and purpose. Despite Jonah's illusion that he can flee from the presence of the Lord, it is now made obvious that God is there on the sea, and able to control it, whatever Jonah may think. Jonah is like a young child covering its eyes, and thinking that it is unseen. But God is there after all; there in the calling, there in the flight, there in the sea, there in the storm, there in the casting of lots (1:7). In short, God is with us, in turns a comfortable and uncomfortable truth, depending on our circumstance. 'God with us' is, after all, the heart of the Christian message (Mt 1:23), and a central theme of this book. It is just that Jonah, in his sectarian way, hopes it means 'God is with (only) us.'

23. 'up' and 'down' provide a recurring theme in the book: see for example 1:2 (up); 1:3 (down), 1:5 (down), 1:6 (arise – up) etc.

... sent out a great wind into the sea, and there was a mighty tempest in the sea, so that the ship was like to be broken.
The sea, to Israelites and Babylonians alike was the kingdom of death. (For me, a twenty-first century European, it is the air. I hate flying; the more so when visited, like Jonah, with turbulence. Even today, it certainly makes the most pagan people turn to their prayers, see 1:5.) For these ancient peoples, to be floating on the sea is risky enough, to be tossed around worse, and to feel the timbers straining and cracking worse still. The little vessel of security is breaking and the terror of being swallowed and engulfed is growing by the minute. It is partly this almost primal fear of being engulfed that has aroused such empathy with the victims of the 2004 Asian tsunami, the obsession with retelling the story of the *Titanic*, perhaps even the solo voyage of Ellen Mac Arthur. Despite our technology and statistics of safety, it doesn't take much to rock the boat of confidence.

We shall ponder this ship further, but first some more about the terrified crew.

5. Then the mariners were afraid, and cried every man to his god ...
From this little verse, we gain the important information that the mariners are pagans, who cried every man to his god, probably different gods. Much reflection hinges on this. I have already referred to the uneasy 'fellow-ship' and it is very like the church in the world. Jonah, the one with faith in the true God, is mingled with the crew, quite literally 'in the same boat' as everyone else, subject to the same physical forces, hopes and fears and all the rest. As seems always to have been the case, people are tossed around in an uncertain and vulnerable world, and there are many answers given to describe the reason for the dreaded destruction. For Christians, it is common to bemoan the 'great unwashed out there' and to look with self-righteousness at the way the world is going. The assumption is that the world is going down because of the unbelief of so many. But here, the author of Jonah turns this upside down; the ship is sinking because of the faithlessness of the true believer, not because of the errors of the

pagans.[24] The world languishes because of a disobedient 'church', not because of a disobedient world. This point is beautifully made in the text in the next few verses.

... and cast forth the wares that were in the ship, to lighten it of them ...

Notice that, in addition to praying to their pagan gods, the mariners do the sensible physical thing – throwing cargo overboard. But it is the weight of their human cargo that is the problem, and it is this that will have to be sacrificed ultimately to make things calm for them. Also, Jonah himself will have to realise that personal sacrifice will always attend his vocation; in this chapter it is his life; later it will be the laying down of his prejudice. This last he finds much harder.

... But Jonah was gone down into the sides of the ship; and he lay, and was fast asleep.

Humanly speaking, the pagans have been doing what they could, even praying as best they could. In stark contrast, there was no prayer from Jonah, no co-operation on deck, nor even any awareness of the most destructive storm. Jonah is asleep, fast asleep, out for the count. He is paralysed between pragmatism and spirituality, neither a Martha nor a Mary (Lk 10:38ff); his stupor now recalls his condition back at home where he was first wakened by the word of the Lord (1:1). Jonah is ambivalent, neither of the world, nor of God; neither coolly rational, nor on fire for God. He is luke-warm, like so many of us – simultaneously providing an accurate psychological description and evaluation (fit only to be 'spued out')[25] of the crisis of half-hearted faith. A superb commentary on this condition is from the bible itself:

> 'I know thy works, that thou art neither cold nor hot: I would thou wert cold or hot. So then because thou art lukewarm, and

24. We should note however that pagans are people of faith. C. S. Lewis used to say of his unbelieving friends (who described themselves as pagans) that he wished they were – at least they would understand something of faith.
25. See also Daniel Berrigan *The Whale's Tale.*

> neither cold nor hot, I will spue thee out of my mouth.' *Rev 3:15-16*

Unable to settle for either option, Jonah becomes hopelessly inactive and useless between the two. His sleeping shows his indifference to the world of work around him. He is big in ideals but small in social action – in sharp and ironic contrast to the mariners and later the Ninevites who are so quick to translate belief into action (chap 1), faith into works (chap 3). This cameo rapidly raises very contemporary questions of faith and justice; the piety that happily exists independently of social concern or worse, the sort of religion that actually fosters indifference. So Jonah, our anti-hero in his spiritual cocoon (who is not very likeable at this stage in his adventure), is going to need to be disturbed again, this time not directly by God but by the rough and urgent voice of the captain.

6. So the shipmaster came to him, and said unto him, What meanest thou, O sleeper? arise, call upon thy God, if so be that God will think upon us, that we perish not.

Jonah has gone *down* again, and is asked to rise *up*, get off his backside and pray. This is not just any prayer, but prayer to the real God, needed by all on board, mentioned for the first time by the pagan captain, not by Jonah. From the captain's point of view, Jonah's god is only one of many – worth a try – but his understanding rapidly changes in the next verses. There is no indication that Jonah does pray, but the significant thing is that this is the first of many events in the book where Jonah is being woken up to the implications and responsibilities of his own faith.

It is also interesting to see who is responsible for the wake-up call – the pagan captain.

Many times in my life it has been 'non-believers' who have woken me up to what my faith is saying.[26] Here also is the first clue in the book to the role of the believer in the world (currently the microcosm of the ship where all are thrown, and thrown about, together.) But most importantly the same is true *vice versa* – that is, believers need the unbelievers and there are thus the first glimmers of a universal vision and purpose. Chapters 3 and 4 reveal that this universal compassion extends to all people and even animals.

This is a Jewish text, of course, but is profoundly relevant to any world religion that lacks world sympathy or a right sense of Divine priorities. The image of the sleeping Jonah prompted R. T. Kendall to observe that the church, though entrusted with the Word of truth is like Jonah, 'it has looked to Tarshish not Nineveh. The church is like Jonah who paid the fare to sail on the ship going in the opposite direction from what God demanded. The church has spent its energy, its time and money on the wrong things. The church at the present time is like Jonah, asleep in the sides of the ship while the world is tossed in unprecedented bewilderment. The world is afraid – the church is asleep.'[27] This shattering verdict is certainly to be found in the text of Jonah. However, we should note even at this stage that

26. Too many times to record here, and often painfully personal. I have often asked Christian audiences, clergy especially, whether this has also been true for them, and it almost always has.
27. R.T.Kendall, *Jonah an Exposition*.

the other period of Jonah's apparent silence and disengagement from the world's point of view, in the belly of the fish, is anything but inactivity and denial. We shall read of its agonising wakefulness in Chapter 2.

7. And they said every one to his fellow, Come, and let us cast lots, that we may know for whose cause this evil is on us. So they cast lots and the lot fell upon Jonah.
At first sight it may seem paradoxical that the miraculous determinism of the lots, and the apparently natural rationality of the storm turn all concerned to questions of true faith and divine involvement. But there is no separation here of the divine and the natural, and the author has a sure perception of God with us, and all that this means.[28] This theme returns again and again in the book (1:2; 2:1-2, 6, 7; 3:10; 4:10-11); it is the most intimate involvement, even if it never quite touches what Christians might call 'incarnation'. It is of great significance for us in this scientific age, indicating that the natural and rational are not in opposition to God, but part of his creation and action, and through honest questioning are just as likely to lead us to God.[29]

So we come to the *questions*. They begin here – 'for whose cause?', become a torrent in the next verse, and the most searching and revealing of all is found in verse 11, touching the deepest nerves of the interpretation of faith in the modern world. We shall look at them as they occur. In this verse, the mariners want to know what is the cause for the evil that is upon them. The violence of the disturbance has not been assuaged by normal

---

28. This is in itself a fascinating and worthwhile study. God with us, *Emmanuel*, is of course the centre of the biblical story of Christ, but not just to be found in the New Testament. The problem of sin cries out for – but also seems to make impossible – the presence of God. See e.g. Adam and Eve (Gen 3:8ff); Cain (Gen 4:13-17), Jacob (Gen 28:10ff). But for trusting believers, with adversity not of their own making, it is sublimely expressed in Psalm 23:4: 'Though I walk through the valley of the shadow of death, Thou art with me.'
29. There is particular joy in the discovery that in modern physics, reason has driven people to ask questions that reason cannot answer. Physics leads to metaphysics and relationality, upon which all the reasoning itself depends. See e.g. Torrance, T.F.

means, nor even by the passage of time – by 'riding it out'. Indeed, the longer the time and the greater the intensity of the storm, the questions force *super*-natural questions as they move from chattels to persons and their gods – Who (not what) is the cause? It seems, as so often, that they are looking for a scapegoat, someone to blame for this lethal storm. The search for a scapegoat is a sickening quest that re-emerges throughout history and abounds today.[30] Although, it has to be said, the mariners were right in their diagnosis.

The questions intensify:

8. Then said they unto him, Tell us, we pray thee, for whose cause this evil is upon us; What is thine occupation? and whence comest thou? What is thy country? and of what people art thou?

The questions flow thick and fast, because they now have a culprit in the dock before them. Yet it is a trial of themselves also, because Jonah has been tampering with the will of the real true God. One can feel the mariners' growing sense of awe not just at the enormity of Jonah's misdemeanours, but also at the implications for themselves of any answer he might give, and any response they might have to make. They have seen the power of God, now they want to know the facts – the normal process and sequence of evangelism. They knew Jonah was odd and foreign, but they had no idea he carried so much spiritual cargo, how much it would weigh them down and affect them all. They had got rid of the wrong stuff – an irksome mistake. Once again we can see another theme of this book; once called, Jonah cannot help but be a missionary (see comment on 1:1), despite his best efforts to the contrary. Jonah, quite unwittingly, against his most earnest intentions, has precipitated a crisis – and the torrent of questions bear witness to this. They all boil down to this: *Who are you?* This was a question asked of Christ when people were stunned by his apparent normality but also his attendant power (see Jn 8:25 and (wanting to ask the question) Jn 21:12).

30. There has been a resurgence of interest in 'scapegoat theology'. For further study, see, e.g. René Girard.

9. And he said unto them, I am an Hebrew; and I fear the Lord, the God of heaven, which hath made the sea and the dry land. After all this serious questioning in heavy seas, there is more than a flicker of humour as we hear the answer Jonah gives. He answers the question as to his nationality, and affirms the identity of the true God – the God who made the sea and the dry land (and therefore of course could not possibly be avoided by taking to the sea). God is the God of the sea and the dry land – the source of our insecurity and security; in this order, they lead to God. Jonah's quote is perhaps also a piece of Clip Art (derived from Ex 14:21), a standard religious formula, well known to all Jewish people. But again, as Jonah trots out this automatic piety of the true believer, he is slowly being woken up to the implications of what it is actually saying. Most of the time, we almost certainly need the same awakening with our creeds and other religious formulae that trip off the tongue. But the awakening is profoundly important; the new circumstance makes the old truth stand afresh – the substance of living out an ancient faith in a changing world.

Now, here is a Hebrew with all these things, and yet a human being in the same boat. There is much that can be learned from this encounter, and much urgency in the learning, but the sailors stumble first over the paradoxical fact of Jonah's disobedience ...

10. Then were the men exceedingly afraid, and said unto him. Why hast thou done this? For the men knew that he fled from the presence of the Lord, because he had told them.
The sailors see very readily the power of God and the danger and illogicality of not doing God's bidding; it is their voice that makes Jonah see his responsibility. A simple question from pagan mouths jolts Jonah further through wakefulness into consciousness. The sailors, as also the Ninevites in Chapter 3, are rapidly becoming much more converted than the prophet who has had a lifetime and whole inheritance of faith. We may note how often this happens in the church. Yet, with an almost surgical delicacy during his sleep and denial, God is also working to convert the prophet – to bring Jonah gradually to God's way of

thinking. This last is very much harder work for God, taking the book as a whole, as there are engrained presuppositions and established infections that have to be carefully washed away. In the later post-operative phase, after the shipwreck and the journey into the underworld, no more effectively, but much more explicitly, God is intimately involved with a painfully conscious Jonah, reminiscent of Jacob wrestling with God (Gen 11). Disabling him all the while, God will gently force him to lean daily on the very grace and mercy he regrets being applied to others.

We should note that Jonah does not answer the question put to him: Why hast thou done this? So the sailors follow it with another ...

11. Then said they unto him, What shall we do unto thee, that the sea may be calm unto us? for the sea wrought, and was tempestuous.

This question, it seems to me, is the deepest that can be asked of believers, and one that reflects exactly the attitude of contemporary society to the church. The sea is still raging, dangerous and bewildering, and Jonah is an irritating presence, talking a strange language of ancient formulae, yet seeming somehow to embody the answer. Even before we hear Jonah's brave response, we get a scent of what is to come. The stakes have been raised to the level of doubt or faith, storm or calm, death or life; this is no ordinary ferry crossing – yet the choice that affects all rests with the believer alone. The believer is intimately and responsibly connected to the world's drama. By their intense questioning, the sailors reveal our faith (or lack of it), and theirs (or lack of it). The question does not invalidate respect; rather, it indicates it. The issues before us all are so great – is there a true God, what of life and death, of fear and hope, of storm and calm?

But the question is now so *personally* sharp – not 'what shall we do to be saved?', but 'what shall we do *unto thee* to make our turmoil quieten?' This, for Jonah, sharpens both the pain and the privilege of vocation. As was said of Christ:

He saved others, himself he cannot save. *Mt 27:42*

When the passers-by at the cross of Christ taunt him like this, they hardly realise that the two are, of necessity, linked. 'Your loss is my gain.'

Jonah's response to the sailors (1:12) indicates a bravery that makes it quite clear that he did not run away from God because he was afraid for himself. Rather, as we shall see, he was afraid of what God might do in mercy (4:2). We like him more, and less, at this point.

The circumstances that have arisen from his vocation have driven Jonah to this point of bearing witness, confessing his own God (1:9) and his own sin (1:10, 12). These things held together are the foundation of our practical faith. For Jonah, it is his personal witness and it now apparently leads to martyrdom …

12. And he said unto them, Take me up, and cast me forth into the sea; so shall the sea be calm unto you: for I know that for my sake this great tempest is upon you.

Personal questions continue to elicit personal response. Notice first how Jonah is ready to be completely condemned for his unfaithfulness and lose his life. This is very odd indeed unless there was already in his mind a fate worse than death, more to be avoided – again not revealed until Chapter 4. Jonah is more willing to die than to obey God's command to do the unthinkable (4:3). The narrative becomes profoundly Christian at this stage; Jonah is driven to spark in the darkness; in confessing, the way out is found – *to save others but not to save himself*. This is another cost, consequence and privilege of vocation and discipleship.

Yet to kill the prophet is to kill the repository of truth, and you can feel a growing suspicion on the part of the sailors that this may not be a good idea. The Goose with the Golden Egg. But then, not to kill him seems to be worse.

13. Nevertheless the men rowed hard to bring it to the land; but they could not: for the sea wrought, and was tempestuous against them.

Notice now the humanity of the sailors stands in sharp contrast to the segregated religion and indifferent propriety of Jonah up to the point where he finally offers his life (1:12). The men are now rowing, the mast having been smashed, the rudder perhaps broken and the rigging torn. But they could not. They are rowing against the will and purpose of God. Jonah, hardly a helpful hand on deck, does not appear to 'row in' with them, perhaps aware of the futility of it, perhaps unable to see or respond to their decency. In the appalling circumstances, they can see no purpose for good in the gruesome task that lies ahead, so they naturally try to avoid it. Is there any other way? This enacted question by the sailors reverberates through the scriptures, perhaps most clearly seen when Christ will set his face for Jerusalem, and voices of disciples such as Peter[31] and even Judas[32] yearn for something easier, more humane, more obvious. The pressure of the impending sacrifice is unbearable, and one can well sympathise with this. No wonder …

14. Wherefore they cried unto the Lord, and said, We beseech thee, O Lord, we beseech thee, let us not perish for this man's life, and lay not upon us innocent blood: for thou, O Lord, hast done as it pleased thee.

How much theology there is in this agonised cry! Notice that this is the first prayer offered (by anybody) to the true God. The word 'Lord' is repeated three times in this prayer to make the point. Jonah has not yet prayed at all – he has to sink down further for that to begin. The sailors pray that they will 'not perish for this man's life', yet the reverse will be true – he will perish for theirs. They pray, 'lay not upon us innocent blood' even though they will be the ones that take it. Later, the crowd in the Passion story will say, 'His blood be on us and our children' (Mt 27:25) – it was, and it also saved them.

31. 'Surely, not, Lord', said by Peter, shocked by the offence and sacrifice of the cross. And Jesus' response is shattering: 'Get thee behind me, Satan: thou art an offence unto me: for thou savourest not the things that be of God, but those that be of men.' Mt 16:23

32. The 'betrayal' of Judas Iscariot may well be best understood to be motivated by a desire for getting Jesus to go to the highest places, and 'show them all'. See also Vanstone's *The Stature of Waiting*.

... for thou, O Lord, hast done as it pleased thee. Here is the absolute will of God. What is disobedience under the sovereign God? It was the will of God, what else could we do?[33] It is past tense now, there is no other option but the road of sacrifice ...

15. So they took up Jonah, and cast him forth into the sea: and the sea ceased from her raging.

It may be worth asking why Jonah had to be cast into the sea by the sailors, rather than making a suicidal jump. This, in modern language, is assisted suicide, and contrasts nicely with Jonah's voluntary suicidal tendencies in Chapter 4 (4:3, 9). It seems that the action of the sailors combined with the consent of the prophet make for a deeper truth, and, as it turns out, the most perfect timing – from the point of view of the fish.[34] Moreover, as someone has observed, the trouble with living sacrifices is that they wriggle off the altar – and may need help to sustain their intention.

More seriously, there is this to consider: entering into the sea, it loses its power; avoiding it, the sea rages on. This is an almost limitless parable, with parallels in all our lives.

We have said that the sea is symbolic of destruction, swallowing up and death. But, because it is water, it also indicates life. It is thus the point of death and life, if entered with God, who made the land and the sea (1:9). Examples of this two-edged sword might include the flood (where the same water that drowns sin floats the Ark); Moses and the Red Sea (where the same water that saves and distances the Israelites drowns their opponents); and our own baptism of course where sin drowns in the same water that cleanses for new life.

33. The same question is addressed by Peter in Acts (Acts 11:1-17, esp 17b). In the Acts story, it is worth noting that the assessment of God's will is also on physical evidence; again, (as in the Book of Jonah) the permissible extent of Jewish faith to Gentiles is under review.

34. Indeed, we might ask whether the fish would have been there if the sailors had not sought to bring Jonah to land. The import of these apparently silly reflections is that they point to the reticulation of God's purposes, using our best and worst actions to make something to save us. This is a deeply biblical theme, and supremely illustrated by the passion stories. It is also the greatest possible source of hope.

The consequences are remarkable and, whatever about the future of the unfortunate prophet, it is clear that this reluctant phase of his mission is over and yet has been very fruitful indeed ...

16. Then the men feared the Lord exceedingly, and offered a sacrifice unto the Lord, and made vows.

We might well add that Jonah made a sacrifice also – the ultimate sacrifice. However, it is worth noting several important lessons. The men 'feared the Lord exceedingly'. This is not negative fear such as the fear of the storm, but the Fear of the Lord (see e.g. Prov 1:7), full of the best and most intimate connotations of having faith in God. More than that, the sailors respond in practical ways – they 'offered a sacrifice unto the Lord and made vows' – consecration of possessions and persons, signs of complete conversion, and an acknowledgement that God is Lord of both. There is good theology in these new converts. This would not make very happy reading for a narrow-minded believer, because exactly the same virtues of offering and commitment at the height of Jewish faith are now being applied to pagans with no history or culture except seafaring. It is far worse, and really drummed into the reader, when the loathsome Ninevites respond in the same way and they are awarded by God a faith such as Abraham enjoyed.[35] The implications of this seemingly innocent response are enormous; Jonah's God is not the pet deity of one particular nation, but sovereign ruler of heaven and earth.

The mariners get to see and understand this long before Jonah.

But we should remember Jonah also. By his offering, people are snatched from death – not just material death but spiritual also. This is consummated by the offering of Christ.[36] Christ has

35. See Jon 3:10. This is one of the many instances in the Book of Jonah that indicate an interest in how the Jewish religion relates to the rest of the world. This is one reason why Jonah is read at Yom Kippur, the feast of the Atonement.

36. 'What Jonah could not do, but his attitude announces, is done by Jesus Christ.' Ellul p 37.

our sins laid upon him, and he saves us from spiritual and physical death. Jonah was guilty, Christ sinless; how much more does Christ achieve.

Whether we remember Jonah or not, God does:

17. Now the Lord had prepared a great fish to swallow up Jonah. And Jonah was in the belly of the fish three days and three nights.

I was studying this chapter in a cabin on the Irish Ferries superferry *Ulysses* and wondering what the captain's valediction to Jonah might be, 'Do take care, won't you?' or something. Then the following came over the loudspeakers: 'I'd like to wish you a safe and pleasant onward journey.' What a splendid coincidence!

Poor Jonah; his onward journey is anything but pleasant, but it does go onward, leading much further down in fact. Everything will be stripped from him in Chapter 2, except his dependence on God. I suppose the journey was 'safe' enough in this sense, because survival or death is totally dependent on the

Grandmaster's next move. Can the game go on after such a major piece has been sacrificed?

In this verse, the word 'Now' could very well be another 'but', and indeed is translated as such in the NRSV. Certainly, it indicates that although Jonah has disappeared from sight to the sailors, he is very much in God's sights. Jonah goes down for three days and three nights, the accepted duration of a journey to the underworld. We should note that it is a journey, with a destination and a return – in modern language a Three-Day Return. In the hands of God, there is great power in this self-offering.[37] Jonah has been driven to confess publicly his faith *in extremis* and makes the most extreme sacrifice, but by this something totally new and unexpected is born – as developed in the Chapter 2.

The sailors did not know the Lord and yet are clearly seen to have 'done well'. That is, they considered the true concerns of God, and the requirements of all humanity well in advance of Jonah, the 'true' believer (1:6, 10, 13, 14, 16). In elegant contrast, Jonah does know the Lord and does not really care a fig for anything or anybody, least of all himself. God will later question him: 'do you do well ...?' (4:4, 9) The contrast between the obvious humanity of the sailors and the convolutions of Jonah's movements is a salutary parody of the life of faith.

As for the great fish, regrettably the chief thing people remember about the whole story, I am reluctant to comment on probabilities. To attempt to prove it is foolish and needless, though one wry commentator has observed that it might have been possible for the fish to swallow Jonah because he was only a minor prophet.[38] What happens inside the 'belly of the whale' is of course hugely important. Before we turn to this episode, we might ask a couple of further questions that suggest the complex completeness of God's working, whether we co-operate or not.

37. There are strong resonances of the most profound christology here: 'For whosoever will save his life shall lose it: and whosoever will lose his life for my sake shall find it.' Mt 16:25.
38. Quoted in *The Interpreter's Bible: Jonah, Text, Exegesis, and Exposition.*

Would the mariners have been converted if Jonah had not fled the Lord? Would Jonah have begun to realise the geographical and pan-national extent of God's love and providence, without his flight? As we observed at the outset of this chapter, God's word will accomplish.[39]

The humorous ambiguity of this moment of the story, before the serious agonising in the 'whale', is reminiscent of:

A lady bathing on the beach,
Was carried far beyond her reach.
A shark, attracted by the sound,
Just saved the girl from being drowned.[40]

39. St Paul wrestles with this problem of divine providence even when we disobey, and is at pains to point out that we should not therefore sin the more so that grace has to keep up with it. See Rom 5-7.
40. Source unknown, but quoted in R. F. Horton.

Jonah – Chapter Two

Jonah now plumbs the depths of just about everything. His whole world and worldview is submerged and lost from sight, like another flood[41] – and the more he descends and loses, the more we wonder whether he can rise again and find. Yet, as Bishop Jewel observed, Jonah is 'drowned yet touched no water, swallowed up yet not consumed'.[42]

Some scholars have argued that this chapter is misplaced;[43] it certainly is in a different style. But it is integral to understanding the whole book, as we shall see, and as a test of this, you can imagine that the narrative of the whole book is written around this psalm (2:2-9) – much as we might compare our own life with, say, Psalm 23.

In this chapter, Jonah is chastened and is thrown back on God's mercy as never before. It is topped and tailed (2:1, 10) by brief narrative, but verses 2-9 form a profound psalm, or canticle, itself Clip Art more-or-less throughout from many other psalms.[44] Jonah takes the plunge into the most unfamiliar territory – not even territory strictly speaking – which makes it all the more frightening, even though God is God of land and sea. He survives – how much better for the experience is doubtful, but he has certainly entered something akin to the 'dark night of the soul'; many have seen in this psalm a profound comment on their own experience.[45] Every foundation is challenged, re-

41. See Genesis 7, especially 7:23.
42. Jewel, John, quoted in Sasson p 65.
43. See, for example, Sasson, and *The Interpreter's Bible*.
44. Psalms 16, 31, 42, 47, 48, 60, 120, 130, 139, 142. It is very noteworthy that some of these psalms are from the Exilic period (see Introduction).
45. e.g. see Paul Murray's comments in *Journey with Jonah* on Thomas

moved even. In modern language, the rug is pulled from under him.

In fact the chapter does indeed touch on the most central themes of all our lives:[46] death, repentance, mercy, judgement, salvation, even 'resurrection' may all be found in the few verses. The humour of the book is almost lost in the face of such weighty matters, but the situation remains very funny in itself – a lonely prophet singing a canticle in the belly of a fish. Also the irony is still there to be found: Jonah's place of extinction is the place of his recommission, his place of repentance is the place of rebirth. What is not funny is Jonah's agony: acute and terribly real. When he is thrown into the sea, he does not know that God's wrath is a means of showing his pardon and alas, when he does know, he soon forgets or deliberately puts it out of mind – for fear of its logical consequences (4:2).

Jonah has heard God, and doubtless through his tradition knew much about him, but *in extremis* he comes to know God for the first time. This discovery, or re-discovery, of a personal faith reaps the highest rewards, because it carries with it the hope of universal love, and even perhaps salvation (2:9, 4:11).

In the first chapter, Jonah has found that there is a wideness in God's mercy; in this chapter, after taking the plunge, he needs now to find its depth.

1. Then Jonah prayed unto the Lord his God out of the fish's belly,

Until now, Jonah had some quite effective ministry, even in disobedience. This is the mark of the true prophet, where the key factor is the divine election, not the perfection of the prophet (1:1). Jonah's success is despite himself. He has been instrumental in the conversion of a pagan crew who readily respond to God and pray to God. Ironically, Jonah – the man of true religion - has not prayed at all, and certainly not prayed for himself or his fellow passengers, even in a hurricane. Like so many of us, he is

---

Merton and St Columba.

46. 'The agony of Jonah's is in fact the agony of every man.' Ellul, p 51.

driven to prayer by personal circumstance. In the words of George Herbert:

> If goodness lead him not, yet weariness may toss him to my breast.[47]

Now, he finds himself praying for the first time, and in earnest, and in the oddest of places, the belly of the whale. There is more than a flicker of humour in this. The fishy belly will turn out to be more a place of gestation than digestion. But two serious questions arise: whether Jonah's prayer can reach God and whether in the act of praying, Jonah will move on in his relation with God and his self understanding. This process in prayer is central to many biblical prayers, most notably found in the entirety of Psalm 139 where the benign reverie of divine care is brutally interrupted by passionate indignation, only to lead to the deepest heart searching that echoes the beginning of the psalm.[48] That God might hear and answer such prayers, perforated by indignant selfishness, is a wonderful testimony to love.

2. And said, I cried by reason of mine affliction unto the Lord, and he heard me; out of the belly of hell cried I, and thou heardest my voice.

Here it is in print: Jonah's motivation for prayer is revealed by this verse; it stems from his affliction. To be more charitable about what motivates our prayer, I must add that in my own ministry I have found again and again that people find God at the extremes of their grief and pain – the very things that might reasonably suggest that there is no God. This verse assures us that there is a God who does indeed hear, even from places that would seem to be beyond God's reach or concern, and certainly beyond any expectation that could be derived from our own merit. You cannot be lost from God.

To quote again from Psalm 139:

> Whither shall I go from thy spirit? or whither shall I flee from

47. *Gifts of God* quoted from *A Book of English Poetry.*
48. Contrast Ps 139:1-18 with 22-24 and thence with 24-26.

> thy presence?
> If I ascend up into heaven, thou art there: if I make my bed in hell, behold, thou art there.
> If I take the wings of the morning, and dwell in the uttermost parts of the sea;
> Even there shall thy hand lead me, and thy right hand shall hold me.
> If I say, Surely the darkness shall cover me; even the night shall be light about me.
> Yea, the darkness hideth not from thee; but the night shineth as the day: the darkness and the light are both alike to thee.
> For thou hast possessed my reins: thou hast covered me in my mother's womb. *Ps 139:7-13*

Note the paradoxical connection between invisibility, even apparent lostness in the generative mother's womb. Darkness and light are also contrasted well in Jonah: darkness in the belly of the ship and the belly of the whale; light in the visibility of evil (1:2) and the rising of the sun (3:8). All alike, as in this Psalm, are known to God.

The next verse prompts some discussion on the relationship with God, but here we should note the crucial shift from the impersonal knowledge of God to the personal: I cried to the Lord, and *he* heard me; ... and *thou* heardest my voice. This intimacy is sustained in all the next verses during the most graphic descriptions of personal crisis and only reverts to the general description of God's work in verse 9. It is worth commenting on the interaction between God and Jonah. It begins (1:1) with the word from God, precipitating evasive action from Jonah; now (2:1ff) it moves into words from Jonah responded to with action from God. In Chapter 4, words and actions work together on both sides.

To return to Chapter 2, we note that there is no contradiction between personal loss and personal faith, possibly the reverse; it depends on whether God is behind, or in, the loss. This has already been suggested by the narrative (1:1-2:2) it is understood by Jonah and acknowledged in prayer:

3. For thou hadst cast me into the deep, in the midst of the seas; and the floods compassed me about: all thy billows and thy waves passed over me.

It was *thou* who has cast me into the deep ..., despite the fact that the mariners actually did it (1:15). Here, as elsewhere, the thorny question of predestination and free will is unselfconsciously addressed, by narrative rather than analysis. Many religious paradoxes can only be *told,* at two levels, often by statement and counter-statement; they disintegrate or make no sense if parsed or analysed.

In this verse, there is real personal faith and dialogue with God. The words 'thou' (or 'thy') and 'me' occur three times each. Here are the ingredients of real progress and process in prayer. Yet it all happens in the midst of the sea; previously Jonah had thought this to be the place where God is absent, yet now he affirms that it is 'thy' billows (Ps 42:7) and 'thy' waves that pass overhead. Moreover, it is God's deep:

Out of the depths have I cried unto thee, O Lord.
O Lord, hear my voice. *Ps 130:1*

... here, in the depths, is a place where there is real death, humanly speaking. It is totally beyond human power to rectify or redeem, but it is not the same as absence from God. Rather, it is dependent upon God in an essential way – there is no-one else, not even self, who is reliable. One can only cry for mercy; in the end, in the hour of our death, there is but this cry.[49] In this apparent contradiction lies the whole Christian hope. The place of extinction and nothingness can only be redeemed by contact with God; God who creates from nothing (*ex nihilo*) speaks into nothingness and forms new life and hope.

Consequently, it is amid the sickening waves of fear and dread that it is possible to be in touch with God – and this with previously unparalleled depth and necessity. There are the most resonant evocations here of the crisis that Jesus was later to face

49. This is the substance of the Jesus Prayer: 'Lord Jesus Christ, only Son of the Living God, have mercy on me, the sinner.' Cf also 'Hail Mary ... now and in the hour of our death.'

in Gethsemane where there is a powerful description of lonely and overwhelming dread:

> And they came to a place which was named Gethsemane: and he saith to his disciples, Sit ye here, while I shall pray. And he taketh with him Peter and James and John, and began to be sore amazed, and to be very heavy; And saith unto them, My soul is exceeding sorrowful unto death: tarry ye here, and watch. And he went forward a little, and fell on the ground, and prayed that, if it were possible, the hour might pass from him. And he said, Abba, Father, all things are possible unto thee; take away this cup from me: nevertheless not what I will, but what thou wilt. *Mk 14:32-36*

Stripped eventually of the vigilance of human company, Jesus shares a vitally necessary personal intimacy with God alone. His I-Thou dialogue is not lost, at least until the last words from the cross: 'My God, My God, why hast thou forsaken me?' Yet even there, the redemptive contradiction is maintained – How can he address God if God has forsaken him? How can God respond to what he has abandoned? Herein lies the heart of the life-giving paradox of our faith. In Gethsemane Christ says, 'Thy will be done', recalling his own prayer he taught the disciples. Jonah will also say this, though his acceptance of God's will is certainly not based upon consent.

4. Then I said, I am cast out of thy sight; yet I will look again toward thy holy temple.

'... I am cast out of thy sight': Jonah thought death was preferable to obedience; now he approaches seeing what death is like. Later, even with this dreadful experience behind him, he will still wish for death if, from Jonah's point of view, God persists in doing the wrong thing (4:3, 8).

In his experience of real dereliction, he has tasted what it is like really to believe that you are out of God's sight and knowledge or care. In reality it is terrifying, but the irony is that it is the very thing he has been desiring (1:3, 10) – as he dedicated himself to fleeing 'from the presence of the Lord'. Here and elsewhere in the book (4:8), God gives Jonah a taste of what he thinks he wants, either for himself or for others, as an adult might to an implacable child, 'all right, try it if you must – you won't like it!' Here in fact are more signs of Jonah's childishness, culminating in the almost total regression described in chapter 4. Jonah and his predicament express perfectly the believer's dilemma of wanting to be in the presence of the Lord, and yet finding it too much the more real it gets. Much of the Old Testament is full of this sort of thing: for example Moses' encounters with God (Ex 3:5, Ex 19). The unapproachable holiness is implied also in much poetry – e.g. T. S. Eliot's *The Four Quartets:*

> Human kind cannot bear very much reality.

Here also is the complaint of Cain after his banishment: 'my punishment is greater than I can bear.'[50] The closer the company with God, the more sharply is defined our sin. Banishment is the only option, but it rapidly becomes unbearable when it happens.

'... out of thy sight; *yet* ...' There is an hiatus, a moment of turning, in the middle of this verse, like the mathematical position of stasis at the top (or bottom) of a parabola. Yet as Jonah recalls this moment in his prayer, we can see that it is the end of his flight and the beginning of the return. It is deeply resonant with other examples in scripture, most notably the Prodigal (or Lost) Son. Again motivated by loss:

> When he came to his senses, he looked again towards home.[51] *Lk 15:17*

When Jonah begins to experience the pain of the separation he so much wanted, his thoughts first turn back to God '... yet will I look again toward thy holy temple'.

Actually, he 'looks' back to home. It is a wonderful human capacity that we can contemplate from a distance, and elect to

50. Gen 4:13-16, especially 16: 'Cain went out from the Lord's presence.' Note that God puts a mark on Cain which, like the Cross of Christ, is a sign of sin but also of protection, of judgement but also of mercy. This story and many others in Genesis, indicate the reality of sin, but also the provision of God. It is supremely seen in Christ.
51. For the whole story, see Lk 15:11-31.

travel towards what we see in our 'mind's eye'. We can also look to the past and reflect in remembrance (2:5-8). Holding to this vision of 'homecoming', he describes in the next three verses the remembrance of real depths to which he has fallen. This juxtaposition is most starkly expressed in verse 7, as we shall see. Unfortunately, when Jonah finally returns, the homecoming just re-presents the problems he has had prior to his flight.

5. The waters compassed me about, even to the soul: the depth closed me round about, the weeds were wrapped about my head.

According to the Hebrew, Jonah is up to his neck in it, but actually he is submerged more thoroughly than this (2:6). Here is the first mention of the real and total death – not just of the body, but also, as translated, the soul. Herein lies the ultimate terror. Returning to Gethsemane:

> 'Jesus saith unto them, My soul is exceeding sorrowful unto death: tarry ye here, and watch'. *Mk 14:33*

We might also note the thing Jesus warned us to fear above all things:

> And fear not them which kill the body, but are not able to kill the soul: but rather fear him which is able to destroy both soul and body in hell.' *Mt 10:28*

Here is the moment, not just of utter helplessness, but of entering the blackness irrevocably – once and for all. Jonah's *soul* up to now has been hard to find; he has been ready with religious formulae but not with their applications or solutions. Here too is the truth that makes this book so relevant for us now, when all the values to which we cling so tenaciously are stripped from us. This is when religious or national values upon which we are founded, *founder*.

6. I went down to the bottoms of the mountains; the earth with her bars was about me for ever: yet hast thou brought up my life from corruption, O Lord my God.

'... I went down to the bottoms of the mountains ...' The descent continues, like Alice in Wonderland, but there is no soft landing, no solution, no remedy to drink.

In this position, in a sense Jonah has hit bedrock, but there is a unique mercy to be discovered deep down here. This is the sort of relief we find when we finally admit that we have no power of our own to rescue, and are forced to trust others – for example in the moment of surrender when being put to sleep before a medical operation.

The mercy here is that the sea (with all the connotations of destruction that it had) is undergirded by land – wholesome and solid. The two have become one, or rather the sea is just a pocket in the land. This bedrock, like Christ himself, is where all things connect.

Underneath are the everlasting arms. *Deut 33:27*

Thus '... the earth with her bars was about me for ever ...' or in modern language, *Davey Jones' Locker*, might be seen paradoxically as a mercy, locked on a secure and eternal foundation. The moment of entrapment is the beginning of liberty, paradoxical though it seems. (Consider the second Collect from Anglican Morning Prayer: '... whose service is perfect freedom'.)[52] In this place, Jonah has totally entered the area of otherness – first it was the pagan sailors and their voyage for Tarshish, now it is depths of the sea – later it will be the great city of Nineveh. Encountering alien otherness is one of Jonah's great problems throughout the story. But the irony is that in the end he prefers physical otherness here in the sea to the human otherness of Nineveh.

Again, Jonah's experience suggests one of the deepest questions, 'Can God be there?' and also: 'Is the God who is with me there through me? Am I therefore the agent of God's inclusion?' There are awesome responsibilities here for the believer – and a possible rationale for mission. Perception of this comes most authentically from the deepest places. Jonah affirms the answer: '... yet hast thou brought up my life from corruption, O Lord my

52. *Book of Common Prayer* 2004, p 96.

God'. He is now reflecting on the reality of this sort of discovery of God. God is there but will not leave us there.

Again looking back, Jonah realises the submerging has touched his soul. But now it too seemed to be fading away and dying ...

7. When my soul fainted within me I remembered the Lord: and my prayer came in unto thee, into thine holy temple.

Here is the ultimate threat of corruption – damage to and loss of the soul. It is at this point of total helplessness that there remains one hope only – to remember the Lord. At the point of physical death, the spirit can yet cry for this soul-mercy, this reception by God, portrayed in all its agonising intensity by one of the robbers crucified with Jesus – 'Lord, remember me when thou comest into thy kingdom.'[53] The great act of remembrance, the Eucharist itself, is founded on this dual remembrance – in our remembering of Jesus, he remembers us.

> *Remembrance* is the deliberate calling to mind of things known in the past, an imaginative summoning that transforms the present, and changes the future. It makes present the past, brings light into darkness, hope into despair. It does not change the circumstances, but it changes the outlook. It seems to be a gift that humans have uniquely – the deliberate use of memory to illuminate and transform. The power of this gift is seen in many ways, for example: field Eucharists for soldiers before going into battle, or relatives round a hospital bed. 'Finally, brethren, whatsoever things are true, whatsoever things are honest, whatsoever things are just, whatsoever things are pure, whatsoever things are lovely, whatsoever things are of good report; if there be any virtue, and if there be any praise, *think on these things* ... and the God of peace shall be with you.' *Phil 4:8-9 (italics mine)*

Now comes the glorious and central affirmation: '... my prayer came in unto thee.' It got there! We have to stand back and pause to realise its import. Despite everything, despite the flight across the waters, despite the submarine voyage to the bottom of the sea, despite the helpless indifference, despite the outright disobedience, Jonah's personal prayer comes to the heart of God. Despite the manifest unholiness of Jonah's actions,

53. Lk 23:42.

his prayer comes 'into thine holy temple'.[54] This is the surest proof that Jonah's vocation is still intact. As before, in verses 2, 3 and 4, the prayer is not at all abstract – the I-Thou relationship is as clear as ever. So aware is Jonah of this crucial relationship that he now vividly sees the futility not just of fleeing from God but also for following roads that lead nowhere ...

8. They that observe lying vanities forsake their own mercy. This short verse is difficult to understand. If it is a comment on his former life, Jonah is admitting that his road to nowhere was bad enough, and worse if he realised that there really is a road to somewhere, and he had missed it. But to my mind there is a bit of the old Jonah in this verse: once he has personally recovered, he is looking sharply out at others, observing accurately their predicament, but not showing any indications of pity, or inclination to help. (Again, the right truth, but held in the wrong way! This is splendidly brought out in the beginning of the next verse, But I ...) This invidious attitude of those who are being saved is a perennial theme in scripture: 'What is that to you?' *Jn 21:22*; 'I thank you God that I am not as other men ...' *Lk 18:11*. It requires correction and sometimes rebuke.

Despite his attitude, what exactly is Jonah observing? Jonah has discovered the saving power and mercy implicit in a personal relationship with God, and he sees all else as vanity. Pride (vanity) is, after all, the original sin, the opposite of relationship, of community. The substance of Jonah's sin in chapter 1 is to be found in his trying to do without God, apart from God. It is his attitude, not his action. Lying vanities can give us all sorts of things we might need, but not the one thing we most need, God's mercy and the fellowship that accompanies it. The linkage of all these thoughts is somehow found in the nature of God as Trinity, and it may be worth digressing to try to connect them.

54. The principal gifts of God travel: faith travels to God; hope travels to the future; love travels to other.

The Trinity has each partner in absolute interdependent communion. Pride, isolation, is the opposite of this: saying, in effect, 'I can do without you, without your instruction, protection, even prohibition.' The story of Adam and Eve and the Fall in Genesis 3 reveals clearly that their sin is not primarily in the actions they do, but the attitude they have. It is not that their separation arises from doing naughty things. It is not that picking the forbidden fruit is sinful; it is the attitude that thinks God need not be considered, can be avoided, even hidden from. Isolation is sin – the very opposite of the Trinity where communion with otherness is essential. It works with people as well, made in God's image – thus, 'it is not good for man to be alone' (Gen 2:18) – yet this is exactly what Jonah sought, alone from God, and from the sailors, until circumstances forced his hand. Jonah is the Fallen prophet. It is perhaps worth noting that we make a great virtue out of 'preserving our independence' for as long as humanly possible, and it is indeed hard to fault this. Yet, we are made to be most ourselves in dependence on others. The perfect story of this is in the story of Jacob, the self-seeking cheat who slowly learns dependence on God, and is finally disabled by wrestling with God – forced thereafter to lean on others (Gen 32:24ff).

Jonah benefits from God's personal fellowship now; later he will begrudge it to others. It is most wonderful that even the path of vanity can lead us to God, once we realise like the Prodigal Son, that it is a road to nowhere, and turn. This is the cause of the deepest thankfulness ...

9. But I will sacrifice unto thee with the voice of thanksgiving; I will pay that that I have vowed. Salvation is of the Lord.
Not like other men, thank you very much, Jonah does the right religious thing, something he later will resent intensely with the Ninevites. However, he is *thankful*, a great virtue in itself, and paradoxically his thanksgiving has arisen out of extreme stress. 'Salvation is of the Lord.' In many ways, these five words are the whole focus of the book, the hinge on which it turns. As soon as he begins to grasp this truth, Jonah begins on the path to physical freedom (2:10). Psychological and religious freedom are never achieved for Jonah, (chapter 4).

We should note that Jonah is not thrown up on the shore beore he has understood two important things to be true for him: he cannot do anything to escape God, and neither can he do anything to rescue himself. These facts are the twin necessities of grace – which now expresses itself in such a funny and bizarre way:

10. And the Lord spake unto the fish, and it vomited out Jonah on the dry land.
It seems the fish was only too happy to get rid of its emetic prophet and finish its mission in such projectile style. Jonah is now on *terra firma* once more and ready for the next adventure.

If Jonah did not die himself, we might well ask, '*What* actually died in this chapter?' The fish seals the extermination and the salvation of Jonah; the deadliest things die, the way to life is revealed. There are indeed threads that pass through mortality without dying, much as light rays, focused by a lens, pass through a theoretical point of no magnitude, only to expand eternally. So, what dies? The option to ignore vocation and, though Jonah never capitulates on this, the option to ignore grace, mercy and peace for self and for others.

Jonah had been glad to be off God's map, and is now glad to be back on it, though still uneasy about the directions it will indicate.

It would seem that there are two things worse than death: death without God, and death of God.[55] Jonah, religious but free, chooses absence from God, and has it granted; in his voluntary exile he finds the concomitant, voluntary hell, intolerable.[56] Thus, with supreme wit, the writer of Jonah shows that this hero gets (by choice) as near to hell as anyone else in the story, even the Ninevites (chiefly by ignorance, 4:11). To the fate of the Ninevites we turn in the next chapter.

55. This last, the death of God, has taken a new popularity with Philip Pullman's brilliant trilogy *His Dark Materials.*
56. The fall of Lucifer, in Milton's *Paradise Lost*, is willing, freefall: he was not pushed.

Jonah is now regurgitated but not reformed; the question to defeated, lost Israel remains: is there a commission, can there still be a commission, a role for God's chosen messengers after such trauma? Can it ever be the same? Can there really be a mission to the Gentiles? Is this what it means to be chosen?

Jonah – Chapter Three

In chapter 1, Jonah saw God in the face of strangers, but he has yet to see God in the face of an enemy – indeed a sworn enemy.

Jonah still has missionary work to do, and the whole question of evangelism floats over the next two chapters. Jonah's evangelism thus far has been successful, despite his efforts to the contrary but we should note that he has also been evangelised himself. Evangelism is not (nor should it ever be) just a case of the 'haves' telling the 'have nots'. Indeed, with exquisite irony, it has been the 'have nots' telling the 'haves' what they have (1:6-10).

As already indicated, the place, the time, the message, the election and the vocation are all from God. Until now, Jonah's chief objection has been the place, Nineveh. But there are more apparently subtle but deeply entrenched objections yet to be revealed.

After his appalling experiences thus far, Jonah is as it were baptised, converted, even obedient (through lack of choice) in a sort of way . Yet he still is deeply sectarian, and has much to learn. He is on the track, but not very far along it. More importantly, he is not happy with where it leads; this dilemma is the most paralysing of our faith – the very thing that repeatedly makes Jonah sleepy, angry or straight disobedient. The liberty of God threatens our most cherished presuppositions, especially religious ones.

In short, as Ellul has said, Jonah is no plaster saint.[57] Though he might wish to be, he is not petrified in his niche; neither can

57. '(Jonah) is still in our image. He is not perfect. He is capable of anger, self-justification, and despair. He has not become a plaster saint.' Ellul, J., p 71.

his true nature be brightly painted over by stylised benevolence. Thank goodness for this; Christian believers likewise are not little creatures of perfection (quite the reverse, many would say) even, perhaps especially, when similarly chosen, converted, commissioned, chastened and corrected. Jonah's vocation, even his re-vocation as he now stands on the seashore, is not equal to perfection – it is just that he is still called, still chosen. God's work does not wait for perfection, but works through fallibility – a repeated theme of this book. One might ask whether this is comforting, or challenging – or both. One of the most marvellous aspects of Jesus' election of his disciples is just this realism, this working with imperfection, and the crowning glory is the assertion to Peter that he is the foundation of the church, wobbly yet corrigible. (To see this, refer to the gospel accounts of Caesarea Phillipi and the passion narratives. Peter has moments of supreme and truthful insight, yet also tells lies and makes awful blunders, e.g. Mt 16:16-23, 26:31-35, 69-75.)

1. And the word of the Lord came unto Jonah the second time, saying,

Poor Jonah hardly has time to wash himself clean before that disturbing word of the Lord comes to him again, as it did in chapter 1. Jonah has sensed the 'outreach' of God, both without and within. He has sensed that God's purposes are meshed together to do all sorts of things simultaneously: to take the example above, God has been simultaneously been evangelising the evangelist and the evangelised. Jonah has sensed a common humanity with the sailors. Through all this, it is the same Lord, the same Word, and very much the same Jonah – still the first-class bigot. There is no mention of mercy in his heart, or willingness in his feet. Indeed, one suspects that his feet were not the 'lovely feet' of those who bring good news (Isa 52:7). As we shall see in the final chapter, Jonah wanted to bring bad news, not good. Yet through it all, he has no option but to hear, and this time to obey. We might note that here Jonah is once again feeling the two-edged comfort of Psalm 139: 'You hem me in, behind and before, you have laid your hand upon me.' St Augustine's dictum also comes to mind, 'our hearts are restless until they find their rest in thee'; but Jonah has a long way to travel before he can rest.

Under God's direct and personal guidance and calling, the narrow man has only narrow options. So, what does he hear?

2. Arise, go unto Nineveh, that great city, and preach unto it the preaching that I bid thee.

The *Jerusalem Bible* translates this very nicely as: 'Up!', he said, Go to Nineveh ....' There is no rest for Jonah. You can imagine him hearing the command to get up, but then, on hearing Nineveh mentioned, thinking 'O God, not them again.' Will God not wise up, get real, give it a rest for a while? But the implacable imperative of God is sustained: 'What's it going to be this time, Jonah, Nineveh or Nineveh?' The reference to that 'great city' is repeated in 1:1 and 4:11, the first and last verses of the entire book. In all three places they carry a sense of importance – importance to God.[58] For this reason the Ninevites' sin is important (rising up to him), and so is their rescue. There is a truth here – God could overlook their sin if the Ninevites did not matter to him. Parents correct the child they love, and for this reason.

We should note that in the first calling (1:2), Jonah is asked to cry against the wickedness of Nineveh. But here he is given no message ahead of time; the word will be given when needed. This is reminiscent of the words of Christ to his disciples, facing into opposition:

> But when they shall lead you, and deliver you up, take no thought beforehand what ye shall speak, neither do ye premeditate: but whatsoever shall be given you in that hour, that speak ye. *Mk 13:11*

Possibly also, the message given (3:4) would have put Jonah off the track for the second time, because when it came it carried more than a hint of repentance. Or it may be that this is a welcome sign of a greater intimacy between God and Jonah than

58. Lit. 'great before God' the strongest form of superlative in Hebrew.

was noticeable in the first calling (1:1-2). After all, they have been through a lot together.

3. So Jonah arose, and went to Nineveh, according to the word of the Lord ...

Jonah now appears to be the obedient prophet. Certainly his actions are in tune with the word of the Lord, but there is no evidence of any change of heart. Jonah, despite having said the 'psalm' in chapter 2, and therefore most definitely knowing his personal need for mercy, will continue to be resolutely non co-operative when confronted with yet more Gentile pagans, much as he was in the ship in chapter 1. It is as if he knows it all, but doesn't; the text but not the meaning; the letter but not the spirit, the actions but not their proper motivation. He is so sure of his election, so lost in the words of religion and the inheritance of his national identity, that he cannot make religion truly apply to himself and certainly not extend to others. Here indeed are echoes of the Pharisees, and many of the nastier outlooks that stalk our sectarian world. Jonah is obedient only to the dictates of circumstance; motivated only by the impossibility of standing still or running away.

... Now Nineveh was an exceeding great city of three days' journey.

Yet again, we are reminded that Nineveh is an exceedingly great city. How great is hard to define, since excavations have not revealed anything like a city that would take three days to cross. This could be argued until the cows come home –and wear sackcloth (3:5), but the uncertainty proves the point made in the Introduction, namely that the places, times and other details have a meaning more than a reality. So let us be reminded of the meaning:

Nineveh was the stylised epitome of evil. You can be absolutely sure that it would be firmly in the middle of President George W. Bush's 'Axis of Evil'. More than that, the king and his nobles (3:7) would be the Ace of Spades and other high cards in the notorious Pack of the Most Wanted – wanted dead or alive.

The three days, (and the forty days in the next verse) are there for their religious importance. Just as Jonah has made a journey down into his own internal hell for three days (chapter 2), he now makes a lateral journey into the hell generated by others. It is a journey into another underworld or, as we might say, underground world of the city. The seed of the word must be planted in the very depths of this alien, Gentile soil. Just as he reached the roots of the mountains (Jon 2:6), he enters the deepest reaches of corrupt Nineveh. Once again, the great question is whether God can be found there, whether anything good and wholesome can germinate in places that seem totally to contradict God's presence. Jonah can accept this for himself, but will refuse it for others – 'nothing is impossible for you, O God, but O God, is it wise? Or right?'

We have noted that Jonah's journey thus far has been like a railway ticket – a three day return; outward and return to the same place. We have yet to see whether this is possible for the Ninevites, who seem to have travelled irrevocably in the wrong direction; the irredeemable in a place of no return. The 'greatness' of the city may emphasise the impossibility of saving it, but equally the importance of so doing.

4. And Jonah began to enter into the city a day's journey, and he cried, and said, Yet forty days, and Nineveh shall be overthrown.

So Jonah has been given his short message at last. In all probability, we might imagine that he will be pleased to deliver it. On the face of it, it appears to be a straight prediction: yet forty days and Nineveh shall be overthrown. But there several snags, as Jonah knows only too well:

In the first place, he is uttering *prophecy*. This, although expressed as prediction of the future, is only prediction if there is no change. It is what will happen if we do not change; warning with a view to avoidance. Then there's a worse problem from Jonah's point of view – that God has a predisposition to be merciful (4:2). Worse still is the unthinkable thought that the Ninevites just might turn. This would mean that repentance

would be granted to the Gentiles with Jewish faith to accompany it. Worst of all is the snag in the message itself that would not be lost on Jonah as a good and God-fearing Jew – the thing about forty days. Forty has immense significance in biblical terms – the flood, Moses[59] – and of course in the Christian stories of Jesus in the wilderness.[60] In all these, the time of testing is also a time of opportunity; it is two-edged. The same water that drowns sin floats the Ark. The judgement of God is not just a pronouncement that stays for all time. The judgement of God is not just a verdict – it makes something, it is creative – and forty indicates that this is just the sort of business that God is about.

Yet it remains that Nineveh shall be overthrown. This is the very message that Jonah most wants to deliver and to see executed, but the very one he least wants to deliver in case it goes tragically wrong. The crisis is precipitated at last, by the word delivered in the place it most needs to be heard. By human agency the divine seed is finally planted where it should be, in fresh, even if alien and sinful, soil. Germinate it must (Isa 45:23) but how will it come up? What will happen now? Everything in the story hinges on this moment. The narrative is splendidly matter-of-fact, as if speaking of an inevitability. The inevitable and the impossible combine beautifully perhaps to our eyes, but in a way that is deeply shocking to the sectarian Jonah ...

5. So the people of Nineveh believed God, and proclaimed a fast, and put on sackcloth, from the greatest of them even to the least of them.

There is much in this verse, but the most startling in the insouciant use of Clip Art where 'the people of Nineveh believed God'. This phrase is very like the one used of the great Patriarch and paradigm of faith – Abraham himself![61] This is the faith that was credited to Abraham as righteousness, the quality of faith that made possible comfortable communion with the Almighty God – so holy that even his name could not be pronounced. This is the beautiful, absolute and central core of Jewish religion, and it is now being shamelessly applied to the worst of the Gentiles, and the most hideous enemies to boot.

Nineveh believed God. Those three words are truly divine –

59. See also 1 Kings 19:8.
60. See e.g.Gen 7:4, Ex 24:18, Deut 10:10, Lk 4:2.
61. Gen 14:6, Heb 11:7-9.

juxtaposing total opposites, reminiscent of the huge power of the 'Word became flesh' of John's gospel.[62]

Worse than this (from Jonah's point of view), they don't just believe, but they show it by their actions. Beginning in this verse and ending in verse 9, the response of the Ninevites is as broad and deep as it could possibly be. Here are both the sentiments and the signs of profound repentance. In this verse, from the greatest to the least of them, the people proclaim a fast, and put on sackcloth. It is not the fad of a select few with hyperactive consciences, not the province only of the religiously disposed, but universal. If you walk through a great city today, and try to imagine *all* the people you meet repenting, wearing sackcloth – it is as hilarious as it is improbable. That's not to mention the sweltering animals (3:7) under a Middle Eastern sun that later causes such grief to Jonah (4:8).

It is a very long time since this has happened for Jonah's people, lost in their own sense of grievance. Now it is as if the author of the book is gently saying, 'when did you last repent like this?' For the people of Nineveh, it is brand new. It is remarkable how when listening to a sermon on grace, a habitual attender can be totally unmoved, but the first-time visitor in the adjacent pew is totally gobsmacked, undone.

But there is more to come ...

6. For word came to the king of Nineveh, and he arose from his throne, and he laid his robe from him, and covered him with sackcloth, and sat in ashes.

The repentance is indeed thorough, broad and deep, from the very greatest to the very least. The breadth is seen first in the response of the people (3:5), and now the king himself responds likewise, acknowledging his subjection to the King of kings. For robes he substitutes sackcloth; for his throne, ashes. These are external signs of profound internal repentance.

---

62. Jn 1:14. The prologue of John (1:1-18) is also preoccupied with the paradox of grace given but not recognised or received by 'his own', and freely given to all (Jew or Gentile) who receive him, entitling them to become children of God (1:10-13).

Moreover, the king exemplifies what happens to us when we become aware of our sin – our metaphorical thrones and robes become abhorrent to us, totally inappropriate. This is an *Old Testament Ash Wednesday*. Earlier, Jonah has been dethroned by the disturbing word of God. Now, by the same means but a very different route, the Ninevites have been brought to the same state before God:

> I have sworn by myself, the word is gone out of my mouth in righteousness, and shall not return, that unto me every knee shall bow, every tongue shall swear. *Isa 45:23*

All, including the prophet (and this is deeply uncomfortable for him to acknowledge) are now on the same ground before God, and equally reliant on God's mercy only. There is nothing else left (2:8; 3:9).

The king is not stripped of his earthly authority, however, and he now uses this to extend the repentance still further, detailing the fast, and even including the animals ...

7. And he caused it to be proclaimed and published through Nineveh by the decree of the king and his nobles, saying, Let neither man nor beast, herd nor flock, taste any thing: let them not feed, nor drink water.

We now have an absolute fast, total and universal. No food, no water; no excuses, no exceptions.

Everything material is offered, as when the sailors were casting the wares into the sea (1:5), and Jonah offering to be thrown into the sea (1:12). The religious Jew, the decent pagan and now the wicked Ninevite all respond in what is ultimately the same way. There is nothing left to hang on to, to keep things afloat, no handle, no grip, no status, no possession – just the hope of mercy. Thus it is here that the king turns to prayer, as Jonah and the sailors have done before him ...

8. But let man and beast be covered with sackcloth, and cry mightily unto God: yea, let them turn every one from his evil way, and from the violence that is in their hands.

The sailors in chapter 1 responded with the material and the spiritual, consecrating persons and possessions (1:16). Now the king's decree takes this further and in this little verse there are all the ingredients for repentance and faith, the twin pillars of Christian and Jewish religion. Let me demonstrate:

All are covered with sackcloth. This is the sign of *repentance*, as we have seen. It is also a cover for nakedness, as in Eden. But it is only a sign thus far; the sackcloth might simply be covering shame, not signalling penitence. But all are also to 'cry mightily unto God'. This is *faith*. This is the sort of prayer that both the sailors and Jonah himself have been driven by God's actions to express. Here, the Ninevites are driven by God's judgement, but the resulting necessity is the same. The Ninevites, as the sailors, are appealing directly and personally (everyone, singly and together) to God. They are not appealing to identity and religious inheritance – as Jonah tried to do (1:9).

All are to turn from their evil way. This is the true repentance, conversion; turning. In Christian language it is *works* – and it is this that God sees (3:10). It is this that signals their readiness for God's desire to forgive absolutely and unconditionally. As the absolution in the Anglican *Book of Common Prayer* has it: 'Almighty God ... desireth not the death of a sinner, but rather that he may turn from his wickedness and live ... He pardoneth and absolveth all those that truly repent.'[63]

So, *repentance and faith, expressed as works* are the prerequisites for receiving salvation from God. This parallels (by contrast) Jonah's own sharp and critical observation in 2:8. This is repentance before God and faith in God. The fruits (works) are seen by God. As remarked in the Introduction, we should note that repentance and faith are not sold cheap in the book of Jonah. If there is a desire for universal salvation, it is not automatic, even with God's desire to show unconditional love. At least in this story it requires the co-operation of the faithful, and the response of the infidel.

63. *The Book of Common Prayer* 2004, p 86.

9. Who can tell if God will turn and repent, and turn away from his fierce anger, that we perish not?

There is only one hope left, but it is the greatest of all, hope in God. The hope is to escape death (that we perish not), the same exactly as for the other Gentiles we have already met – the sailors in chapter 1:14. As with the sailors and Jonah, the Ninevites are saved from spiritual death and physical – separate strands that can never be considered separately, so deeply interwoven are our temporal lives with eternal realities. The common humanity of all, and our consequent vulnerability – whether Jew or Gentile – are never more plainly portrayed.

10. And God saw their works, that they turned from their evil way; and God repented of the evil, that he had said that he would do unto them; and he did it not.

God sees their works – the ultimate sign and proof of inner transformation.[64]

> 'Faith without works is dead.' *Jas 2:26*

They had turned from their evil way, and sought the true way, the way back to God. The destroyers are not destroyed, because they have abandoned destruction. Later, Jesus was to say,

> '... all they that take the sword shall perish with the sword.' *Mt 26:52*

How true this turns out to be again and again in modern life! If you live by the Press, you shall die by it, if you live by offshore bank accounts you shall die by them; the list could go on.

'God repented of the evil': repentance and evil are not two attributes one would normally apply to God. They are perhaps explained more clearly in the *New Jerusalem Bible* by 'God relented about the disaster which he had threatened to bring on them, and did not bring it.'

This chapter reveals many great truths about God, and about people – their life without him, and their response to him. As a whole, the chapter is about transformation, specifically the sort

64. See also Jas 2:14-26.

of transformation that eluded Jonah is his piety and his quest for a quiet life. There is an urgency and thoroughgoing completeness in the response of the Ninevites, in stark contrast to Jonah whose whole religious edifice is collapsing around him – as we shall see in chapter 4.

The means of transformation is profoundly Christian: sin causes the judgement, but the judgement effects the cure. This means that mortality, which sin causes, can become a means of grace. This is one of the divine (grand)master strokes – death is the way to life, not the way from it – at least in God's hands.

Moreover, this truth is universal, for the pious Jew and the violent Gentile. Repentance and faith are for all, not just the special prerogative for Israel. Repentance and faith, turning and believing, corrected error and learning – are the pattern of growth for human beings, in response to each other and to God. By this means humans grow and evolve, corrigible all the while, and death is harnessed in the service of eternal love. For those of us who do believe, election indicates special purpose, not special favour. Here are further indicators of the connectedness of all things, and the influence of faith in the midst of everything .

This influence of faith is beautifully put by Jesus in his short parables in Mt 13. He says that Christians should be like salt, like light, like yeast. *Salt* spreads its preserving and flavoursome qualities and does not require all things to become salt – but its presence infiltrates and stops the whole from going off. Salt cannot stay in the saltshaker, as Jonah wished for himself – it must be spread, distributed, dissolved, sacrificed, become invisible. *Light* does not require everything to change into light, but it must not be hidden. It must travel outwards, illuminating, colouring, shadowing, revealing. *Yeast* cannot stay in the packet – it must be put to work by being thoroughly mixed into the whole. It is not enough merely to activate it; it becomes froth and bubble, but it does not actually do anything – except within itself and for itself, and eventually fizzles out. It has to be engaged, put to work, to exert its true influence. The true privilege and influence of election are only found in the whole lump – this is where, to use a bread-making metaphor, they are *proved*.

Jonah – Chapter Four

It is done. The impossible has happened. What a wonderful transformation! The most wicked people imaginable have turned from their wickedness and lived (3:9). They have found life, faith, hope, forgiveness and, we may presume, joy. Was Jonah pleased? He was not. Nothing is impossible for God – yes – but some things ought to be unthinkable for God. God's action was nauseous to him, and the fact that he, Jonah, should have been an agent in the whole sorry affair was intolerable. Jonah is now a fabulously successful evangelist – a few words in the right place was all it took, and his success signals for him the absolute failure of all that is right and good. Jonah is grapping with theodicy – the question of how and why God acts the way he does – and he cannot easily find an answer. The story of Jonah also suggests that narrative, rather than laboured analysis, is the best way of tackling such questions.

This is one of the most delightful tragicomic episodes in scripture. Perhaps because it is so funny, the narrative travels effortlessly to the deepest places, uncovering the shoddier side of human psychology and revealing profound God-questions of grace and justice.

Let us remind ourselves of where we have reached. Jonah has understood his own sacrifice, experienced Divine rescue, and agreed under duress to be faithful. But he has forgotten, or localised, the grace that made all this possible for him; begrudging it for others, he still hopes for the doom of his enemies. This contrasts completely with the teaching of Christ:

> '... but I say to you, love your enemies, bless them that curse you, do good to those that hurt you.' *Mt 5:44*

This is hard teaching for any of us to swallow and keep down; contrasting nicely with the fish, the unambivalent agent of God (with no free will), who finds Jonah hard to keep down.[65] It is worth noting the contrast between the human and the rest of the natural world. The humans, mariners, Ninevites, Jonah himself, have various free ways of responding. However, with the fish (1:17), the gourd (4:6), and the worm (4:7), God appoints and they respond – the question of whether they like it or not does not arise.

Jonah does not like the way things have developed. You can imagine him muttering indignantly about the Ninevites, 'They shouldn't be allowed to get away with it. Cheap repentance, that's what I call it – as if a few days milling around with long faces and scraps of sackcloth will make up for their evil deeds – and animals, too – the idea of it!' As has recently been said, righteousness is of God, but self-righteousness is a potion of our own concoction.[66] Jonah is still stuck on past injustice, chewing it over and over again, contrasting it with his own religious and national loyalty (1:9). He cannot grasp that God sees what people can become and has blessed the transformation of attitude that makes this all possible.

So in Jonah's case, his carnal nature – so subtly intermingled with his religious profession – has survived, despite new birth. (This reveals the difficulty of being 'born again' as a once-off, as if it were not a daily requirement.) The carnal side is alive and active, but it is not healthy – not so very different from the original evil of the Ninevites. Jonah has got stuck again; paralysed in the most painful way before an idol of God, yet seeing the living breath of God all around him. He cannot see, as St Paul saw many years later, that

> There is no difference: all have sinned and fallen short of the glory of God. *Rom 3:23*

As far as Jonah is concerned (and his concern does not travel

---

65. See Berrigan, D., pp 59-67.
66. From *The Windsor Report – a response from the Inter-Faith Section of the Committee for Christian Unity of the Church of Ireland.*

very far) he has done his bit, and now he wants to get out, or maybe to observe from a distance. But God has not finished with him yet. God is slow to anger and full of mercy; Jonah is quick to anger and empty of mercy. This is no meaningless contrast, futile and without issue; the Divine mercy extends not only to the Ninevites, but also to the bewildered prophet. In this chapter, God evangelises the evangelist, tenderly moving him on in the faith.

1. But it displeased Jonah exceedingly, and he was very angry. Here is another 'but', and the chess game continues. It's Jonah's move, but the Grandmaster will help Jonah to win, whatever way he plays. We are not told the reason for Jonah's massive displeasure until the next verse, so here let us focus on his emotion and attitude – anger. Note that God turns away from his anger (3:10), but Jonah now *becomes* angry; the two are linked causally. Jonah's anger in this chapter signals a rejection of God's will, similar to his flight in chapter 1. There is an implacable divine will behind this, and Jonah realises it. For the first readers of this book, you can see how the decent Israelite would hang himself; he would roar with indignation at Jonah, then, as the roar subsides, would see himself. This is exactly the painful process, the set up, that makes King David see his sin when confronted by Nathan (2 Sam 12). Is God whimsical, or compassionate to deal with us this way? The question is perhaps best answered by asking whether there remains any other way when faced with bigotry so dangerous, so intense and worse – masquerading as virtue.

Jonah has been set up, and is beginning to know it. So he turns to furious, indignant and humourless prayer, not seeing, at all, how ridiculous he has become – yet not losing the intimacy he has established with God in the crisis of the second chapter, and the delivery of the message in 3:1-3. Jonah is strung out across a vast cognitive gulf between knowing what God will do, and accepting that God's will is best. This is made painfully plain in the next verse:

2. And he prayed unto the Lord, and said, I pray thee, O Lord, was not this my saying, when I was yet in my country? Therefore I fled before unto Tarshish: for I knew that thou art a gracious God, and merciful, slow to anger, and of great kindness, and repentest thee of the evil.

Jonah blurts all this out like a cross child,[67] yet there remains an honest, almost Psalm-like dialogue with God. But in the guileless lack of sophistication, his real nature is suddenly revealed.[68] It is only with honesty such as this, however awful, that God can begin his healing work. There is no veneer, no spin, no gloss – just the raw honesty of words spoken in pure anger – unpleasant to hear, worse still to hear yourself uttering, yet their force is in their truth.

'The truth shall make you free.' *Jn 8:32*

It does not have to be cosy; rather better for being the reverse. So, what is the truth, the sorry truth here? Just this: Jonah foresaw the frustrations of his intentions by God. He is disappointed with God, seeing the misapplication of divine mercy as a most unfortunate weakness on God's part.

'Thou art a gracious God ... repentest thee of the evil' is a most significant piece of Clip Art; its provenance is from Exodus 32:14 and 34:6-7, immediately after the shameful episode of idolatry in the worship of the Golden Calf. In the Calf story, there have been times of great uncertainty, and Moses has been away for far too long. In this vacuum, and sense of God's absence, the Israelites fashion something certain, tangible, yet unable to respond – a golden effigy – and begin to worship it. God's reaction, apparently of anger, is not because God is affronted by such a portrayal. It is because, as with Jonah, God cannot bear (and will not permit) people to be captive to a worship and vision of their own making. In love and mercy, God *must* destroy the thing that destroys the evolving life of faith.

67 This *tête a tête* with God has an intimacy about it that is both 'anthropomorphic and sublime' (Ellul).

68. There are many other stunning moments in literature that use the same device, e.g. Evelyn Waugh, *Handful of Dust*, Somerville and Ross, *The Real Charlotte*.

Jonah finds that the word 'gracious' (Ex 34:6) sticks most awkwardly in his throat and he perhaps holds on to Ex 34:7 which says that God 'will by no means clear the guilty'. Like many of us, Jonah cannot tolerate the *unlimited*[69] grace of God. He cannot begin to get his head round something so profligate, unmerited, free. And let it be said, the forgiveness of murderers is very trying for the righteous.[70] Yet the question of theodicy has to face this: grace is unfair, at least in a comparative way. Only by accepting it to be an absolute, irreducible gift can it be understood. Jesus told the parable of the workers in vineyard, to illustrate this (Mt 20:1ff). Note the appellation 'Friend' (20:13) when the owner tries to reason with the disgruntled and hard-working labourers. It is the same approach that we find at this critical juncture in Jonah.

The words 'repentest thee of the evil' might seem strange to us. How can God be said to repent, or contemplate evil? If nothing else, the use of these words to describe even what God might contemplate ought to warn us to be careful in how we use them. In this and other places in the Old Testament, there is no awkwardness in saying that God changes his mind.[71] The idea is that God's will is to lift us out of perdition, but it requires our consent and change of heart. Ironically, neither is easy for Jonah – his religiosity and tight morality stand in the way. It is worth noting also, as Ellul has argued eloquently, that God never repents of the good – a sign of his infinite patience – another theme of this book.[72]

69. The question of limits to divine tolerance or mercy is a very major one in Christian thinking, evidenced recently by the disputes over sexuality in the Anglican church.
70. This sentiment exactly has been a desperately heavy burden in the face of prisoner releases in the Northern Ireland peace process. Only the most secure and well-rooted understanding of a greater purpose than individual 'justice' can justify such measures. For some the pain, very understandably, has quite simply been too great.
71. God does not change his nature, but his response changes in accordance with ours. See for example Ex 32:14, 2 Sam 24:16, Amos 7:3. This is an action dialogue, similar to the prayer dialogues earlier; the persons are the same.
72. Ellul, pp 86 ff. Also 2 Peter 3:9.

3. Therefore now, O Lord, take, I beseech thee, my life from me; for it is better for me to die than to live.

Jonah's disappointment with God is now so deep that he asks for his own death. When his people were the righteous victims of Assyrian brutality, there was at least some compensation in knowing that their suffering was virtuous. Misery but no suicide[73] there. But now there is something infinitely and catastrophically worse: the dissonance between what ought to be and what has happened is still there, but in reverse, and worse still, God is the protagonist. This is what I think psychiatrists call *cognitive dissonance* – here at least it is an unsustainable contrast between all the cherished paradigms of religious life, and the apparent realities of the world, all of which are now being considered under God in the one act of mercy. There is more than a whiff of universalism here, and it is totally 'off limits' to Jonah. This is worse by far than the trip to the bottom of the ocean; *all* security is now lost, not just the physical, but mental and spiritual also.

This heralds a pathetic regression, made very clear in the following verses, as our antihero stamps his foot with rage and bewilderment. He has become a difficult child who has not got his own way.

Jonah's deep perversity is now laid bare; it is perverse in the extreme that Jonah should feel that because of *God's* activity life becomes 'a tale told by an idiot, signifying nothing'.[74] Yet this is what he is saying when he utters, 'It is better for me to die than to live.' Since Jonah has been deprived of seeing the Ninevites die while he is saved, he is saying in essence, 'I'd rather die than see them saved.' (*Them* and *us* is a destructive attitude repeatedly implied throughout the book of Jonah). Yet there is deep theological truth in what he says; the old 'me' must die and cannot live in the new dispensation (4:10, 11). God works with this

73. When I say 'suicide', I acknowledge that Jonah wants to die, but says nothing about wanting to take his own life. This is possibly a distinction without a difference, because the attitude of total futility is the same.

74. Wm. Shakespeare, *Macbeth* 5:5:28.

truth, though Jonah knows not what he says, and perceives it for the wrong reasons. It is through doubt that true faith can be born.

From this we can see once again that God was working on Jonah and Nineveh together and simultaneously. As with the ship in chapter 1, the crew and Jonah both saved each other. All are being saved from paganism, false religion, death and cruelty, to something greater, broader and fairer by far – faith, life and humanity. God is working in and through this world, reconciling all things to himself.

> ... that God was in Christ, reconciling the world unto himself, not imputing their trespasses unto them; and hath committed unto us the word of reconciliation. *2 Cor 5:19*

Before we leave this verse, we should note another piece of Clip Art, miraculously funny and ironic in Jonah's predicament. Jonah's plea for death is startlingly similar to that of Elijah:

> 'It is enough: now O Lord, take away my life'. *1 Kings 19:4*

Jonah is in despair because of his success, Elijah because of his failure.

We might note further that Elijah is 'suicidal' because the *Jews* have *forgotten* God: Jonah wants to die because the *Gentiles* have *remembered* God. Elijah is chiefly sorry on God's behalf, Jonah sorry on his own behalf. There are other parallels between the stories of Elijah and Jonah. Both have divine intervention through the natural world – the storm, the fish, gourd and worm compare perhaps with feeding by ravens, and the broom tree (see comment on 4:6). There are differences between the stories shown up by the similarities: for example, Elijah is in heroic despair, Jonah remains the anti-hero.

4. Then said the Lord, Doest thou well to be angry?

Here is no crude rebuke of Jonah's anger, but rather a question. The word for 'angry' means 'hot'. This is the most exquisitely placed piece of Clip Art, taken from the sorry tale of Cain, after another apparently unfair favour or grace, this time given to his brother, and leading to the most murderous thoughts.

> See Genesis 4:1-16, especially verses 6-7: 'why art thou wroth? and why is thy countenance fallen? If thou doest well, shalt thou not be accepted?' These probing questions stem from Cain's inability to cope with grace. Notice that here, as ultimately in Jonah, God's appeal is to universal kinship – we are all people, related (or at least connected) to one another whether we like it or not, under the one God (Jon 4:11).

The parent-child dialogue continues, as if God is saying to Jonah, 'Are you very angry?'

> It is interesting to see how variously this little verse has been translated: 'You're really angry, aren't you?; You really *are* angry; How very grieved you are, Jonah!; Have you any right to be angry? Does it do any good to be angry? Are you justly aggrieved?' All can be seen as a sort of pastoral reflective listening of parent to child, rather than taunting. 'This is gentle bantering, a rallying of a sulky mind.'[75]

Again, there are resonances with the parable of the murmuring workers in the vineyard (Mt 20:1-16): 'My friend, did I not agree to pay you a denarius?' Once more we are up against the question of grace: the fact that it is unmerited makes it seem unfair. The resolution of this is in the related question of election or vocation. Jonah is *elected to save the whole,* so his implacable anger denies his vocation as much as his flight, perhaps more so. To whom much is given, much is expected (Lk 12:48) – this includes surrender to the Giver, as the gifts work their unpredictable and sometimes unpalatable course. Notice that God, as in the parable, addresses Jonah as a friend, worth rewarding by sharing his thinking, and much as by money. Jonah remains profoundly uncertain – he is definitely the child, and circumstances and the actions of his parent/employer are way beyond his understanding.

Rather, he would like to see the doom of his enemies. But he is no longer involved, and all that is left for him now is to get out and to wait and see what will happen to Nineveh.

75. Prof G. A. Smith, quoted in R. F. Horton.

5. So Jonah went out of the city, and sat on the east side of the city, and there made him a booth, and sat under it in the shadow, till he might see what would become of the city.[76]

'So Jonah went out of the city ...' Jonah is on the move again, but this time with uncertainty. We may contrast this movement with the flight (chapter 1), the entrance to Nineveh (3:4), both *purposeful* whether in obedience or disobedience. But here his movement indicates bewilderment, perhaps especially so in the light of God's unsettling question in the previous verse: 'Doest thou well to be angry?' '... and there made him a booth ...' Jonah does not move far this time; he makes himself a small private grandstand and perhaps is trying, out of harm's way, to become the sole spectator of doom ... till he might see what would become of the city ... He is watching from the side of the sunrise; sheltered, no sun in his eyes, the city under heavenly floodlight, and, he wishes, judgement. Isolated by pride, and desperately lonely, perhaps he is sitting it out – whatever 'it' is. The last time anyone *sat* in the story it was the king of Nineveh; he sat uncomfortably but with conviction in repentance; Jonah settles comfortably, but uncertainly in judgement. Jonah is longer up, or running; he sits down. The king sits inside the city on ashes – the fire of conviction of guilt has already burnt. Jonah sits ouside of the city, well out of it from his point of view, in a place of comfort and safety away from fire and brimstone. Supremely he is out of the place whose people ('them') have caused him ('us') the most shattering vexation and burning anger. This was true at the start of the story but it is even more vexing, after the conversion of Nineveh. They, the Ninevites are the ultimate enemy, the ultimate other. By going out of the city, Jonah also effectively dissociates himself from God's dastardly act of grace; by viewing from a distance he is still hoping that God may yet come to his senses, and

76. We shall take this verse as it comes in the narrative handed down to us, but it is worth noting that many believe it to have been transposed from elsewhere in the text, e.g. as part of chapter 3, when there was still uncertainty as to the divine verdict on Nineveh. However, taking it in this position, it does delightfully throw up the possibility that Jonah is still hoping that God will see sense.

do the decent thing – i.e. destroy Nineveh. Jonah is still a very long way from seeing that the ultimate justice is mercy, setting all free from being bound to the consequences of the past. This is spelled out in 4:10-11.

> The final outcome from Jonah's point of view rests with what happens to Nineveh; the final outcome for Jonah himself (the person) has not yet been reached – indeed is never resolved in this chapter – the parable of Jonah is left without conclusion.

Jonah is a wonderfully absurd figure, sitting there alone in his makeshift viewing gallery, itself an indicator of the frailty of his theological position under God, as are so many of our defences until they are burned to ashes under the implacably benevolent will of the Almighty. In his separation, he has created for himself yet another hell, where his (understandable) prejudice has forced him apart from the place of the mercy of God.

6. And the Lord God prepared a gourd, and made it to come up over Jonah, that it might be a shadow over his head, to deliver him from his grief. So Jonah was exceeding glad of the gourd.[77]
The move and counter-move continues, and now it is for God to do something, but the key truth is not be found in the miraculous provision of the gourd which will rise and fall in a few hours, more rapidly indeed than Jonah's pathetic little shelter in the previous verse. The key is in the word *grief*; God is addressing Jonah's *grief*.

> Grief. This is the same word as in 1:2 (wickedness) and 1:8 (evil). The grief is more than just the frustration of his prophecy; it is the frustration of everything held dear. Here this means Jonah's calamity – his extraordinary crisis of belief, confidence, value-systems, justice, above all the nature of God – everything that gave him identity, energy and reason for living.

Jonah's story is the story of *the chosen person;* it has now become like the story of the fortunes of the chosen people, Israel, waxing

77. It is possible to see how this verse connects more logically with verse 4.

into meaning and waning into futility – at least as measured by military success of the occupation of land. The election by God, the vocation from God, remains the only constant through all the changing scenes of the life of the people Israel; meaning must lie in God, yet Jonah has found that meaningless too. This is real grief, parallel to the episode in the fish in chapter 2, but this time must not be addressed by a simple (if miraculous) rescue mission. Rather, it needs patient talking, thinking, changing of attitude – for which there are no short cuts, cetaceous rescue missions or instant fixes.

So, what of the gourd? Early commentaries rejoice in identifying it as a castor-oil plant, fast-growing and with big and shady leaves. Jonah, in his emotionally wrecked state is exceedingly glad of this provision, as he might have been with the provision of the fish when literally wrecked. Later (4:8), he will be exceedingly regretful of the gourd's demise. But how could such a plant deliver him from his grief? It seems that he has shelter anyway, and the hot wind of verse 8 has not yet begun to blow. One possibility is that the gourd indicates God's caring presence – much as the tender touch of a parent on a cross child; despite the most fundamental dispute and ferocious anger, God is still there for him.[78] The main answer is not given until 4:10. There is certain elegance in this narrative style – opening possibilities and leaving them until their purpose becomes clear (the biggest gap is between the flight in 1:3, the reason for it only becoming apparent in 4:2).

7. But God prepared a worm when the morning rose the next day, and it smote the gourd that it withered.

Here is another 'but', and it is still God's move. Jonah is thrown back on God or nothing and is forced to realise, like the captain (1:6), the sailors (1:14) and the king (3:9) that God is sovereign.

> The Lord gave and the Lord hath taken away: blessed be the name of the Lord. *Job 1:21*

78. This is beautifully described in Francis Thompson's poem *The Hound of Heaven*: 'shade of his hand, outstretched caressingly'. The poem is very strongly reminiscent of Jonah, beginning 'I fled him ...'

Again, easy enough to say, and believe, but sometimes, especially when vulnerable (as at a funeral), near impossible to accept.

These are not capricious teasings or punishments, but object lessons that become necessary where God's wide compassion encompasses greater purposes than individual comfort. The worm has been variously described as 'maggot', 'larva', 'centipede', 'grub' – all revolting and inwardly destructive, and the verb that goes with it implies attack.

> The Hebrew '*watak*' is the same word that is used for the sun that 'beat upon' the head of Jonah, and the wind that attacked the ship in chapter 1. All imply a stress applied by God for his widest purposes.

Jonah is now totally worn out – he was absurdly joyful over the provision of the gourd, and now it too, like all his religious aspiration, has withered. The Lord has given and now the Lord has taken away. He cannot possibly say, 'Blessed be the name of the Lord.'

Worse is to follow, again the 'gift' of God.

8. And it came to pass, when the sun did arise, that God prepared a vehement east wind; and the sun beat upon the head of Jonah, that he fainted, and wished in himself to die, and said, It is better for me to die than to live.

It is hard not to feel sympathy for Jonah again. Jonah is being psychologically tossed to and fro as he was physically in chapter 1 – and again it has to do with his resolute lack of acceptance of the will of God. The sun beats upon Jonah's head and the dry East wind desiccates and saps him, just as the worm sucked the sap and withered the gourd. We have moved inexorably from the removal of external protection to the most psychologically disturbing of all – the removal of the internal – there are now no defences anywhere. He wished *'in himself to die'*. Thus, as in chapter 2, there remains only an utter, naked dependency on mercy. But the mercy of chapter 2 did not rescue Jonah from the contradictions of his mission, and he is no closer here. Previously he wanted to live, but now, knowing the pain of living, he only wants to die. 'Them or me! One of us has to die!' But in these verses (8-11) God says in effect: 'No! All of you must live, by putting to death cruel sin and narrow prejudice.' Both – and together.

> Perhaps also the author is suggesting that God wants to warm Jonah up a bit – to give him some small discomfort – in the direction of the fire and brimstone he so desired for his enemies. It is not difficult to see the parallels here with the 'Golden Rule': 'Do unto others as you would have them do unto you.' A most important lesson for the Pharisaically minded. Perhaps it is as if God were giving a lesson in empathy: 'Shall I show you what you wish for others would feel like for you?'

But at the level of Jonah's broken perceptions, and his overwhelming heat and anger at the futility of everything, there is nothing left but to wish, beg even, for death …

9. And God said to Jonah, Doest thou well to be angry for the gourd? And he said, I do well to be angry, even unto death.

It is hard sometimes to be a believer! Again, here is God's reflective questioning in the face of incomprehension and intransigence. Without a consistent, meaningful God, Jonah desires death. This might be reasonable unless there is a deeper meaning to be found, transcending apparent inconsistency, even capriciousness. It is reminiscent of Job, Ecclesiastes and the Psalms when faced with imponderables. The irony with Jonah is that he finds the greatest difficulty not with human injustice, or natural disaster, but with divine mercy. Poor Jonah! He is now totally reduced, regressed, confused, and victim to the most unstable moodswings. Since there is no answer for Jonah apart from a bewildered decision to choose death, not life, the closing remarks of the book are left to God. Here we do not have divine command, or action, but an invitation to see things from his point of view; a touching plea that itself ends with another question.

10. Then said the Lord, Thou hast had pity on the gourd, for the which thou hast not laboured, neither madest it grow; which came up in a night, and perished in a night …

All your preoccupations, Jonah, ultimately have been to do with yourself – your sense of right and wrong, your religion, your protections, your this … your that. And now you are totally wound up about a simple plant, neither human nor animal, that grew and perished by night.

'Jonah is to learn by his regret for the withering of a useful plant how much more his compassion should be kindled for conscious beings, even children and cattle' (R. F. Horton). One may well argue that this does not deliver from grief either, except as the gate opening to wider mercies which, once recognised, make the anguish seem irrelevant. There are echoes here of Christ's appeal to childbirth as a pain transformed by joy (Jn 16:21). The rise and fall of a humble plant, so obsessively real to Jonah, are indicators of the need to grow in sympathy and imagination, in short, to grow in love. God's love saves Nineveh and now comforts Jonah, not by reassurance, but by disturbance as throughout the book. This is the cost of our freedom; we are not inanimate.

11. And should not I spare Nineveh, that great city, wherein are more than sixscore thousand persons that cannot discern between their right hand and their left hand and also much cattle?

The great truth of these last two verses is that God's deepest motive is pastoral. In giving some of his reasons for sparing Nineveh, God appeals not only to the numbers and greatness – perhaps an appeal to the worth of art and culture, even the greatness of civilisation, but also points out that people do not know their right from their left. In saying this, is God indicating his pastoral concern that the Ninevites are unable to make moral judgements? Thus they are more to be pitied.[79]

Now, if we have not seen it before, we see the central message, communicated by contrast, of the whole story: the absurdity of the scale of Jonah's pity[80] versus God's. The sum of Jonah's pastoral concern is the welfare of a single plant – and that only insofar as it affects his comfort. Contrast this with God's pastoral concern for many people, and to shun wasteful or wanton destruction of a whole city. Indeed, there is a further contrast that we have noted in part before: ephemeral things that might preoccupy us (e.g. the gourd) are contrasted with the permanent, universal intentions of God for humankind, and even animals, too. Later, Jesus will say:

> Labour not for meat which perisheth, but for that meat which endureth unto everlasting life. *Jn 6:27*

We should note once more that we are not told what happened to Jonah; we are just left with a question. There is great wisdom

79. Others, as noted earlier, suggest that this refers to the children of Nineveh – the truly innocent, for whose sake the city is to be spared. There are possibly parallels with God's dialogue with Abraham over Sodom (Gen 18:16-33). This seems quite unnecessary, but is an example of how tortuous exegesis may become when governed by presuppositions about innocence or guilt. See J. Calvin: *Jonah, Micah and Nahum.*

80. It is irresistible not to contrast this with the 'pity of Bilbo' Baggins in J. R. R. Tolkein's *The Lord of the Rings* – an unmerited pity for the detestable Gollum that allows the whole story to go forward and the evil powers to be conquered.

in this; if the story were neatly tied up, then we could put the book down and think 'Well, that serves him right, the little bigot'. But, with the question left open, as in the parables of Jesus, we are forced to question ourselves and ask: 'Does my vision and sympathy tend towards the limits of Jonah, or to the unlimited mercy and forgiveness of God?' Further than this, we have to ask: 'How must the church repent?' Even God is said to repent in this story, so there must be room for change of mind, and heart, for the relinquishment (or at least, expansion) of cherished truths when faced with a greater one; for the transfer of worship of idols to the worship of the ever-living God.

The Book of Jonah outlines the greatest challenges that face the modern world, where religion and nationalism are often the most unattractive partners, willing hideous destruction on those fellow human beings who do not share the same beliefs or identity. National boundaries may be crossed, even broken, by the comings and goings of people. But with religion it is harder because the more diluted it becomes, the more emphatic it feels the need to be; the more threatened the more resolute – and dangerous. This is the *Jealousy of Jonah*.

Contrast this with the eirenic vision of F.W. Faber's great hymn:[81]

> There's a wideness in God's mercy like the wideness of the sea ...
>
> For the love of God is broader than the measure of our mind
> And the heart of the Eternal is most wonderfully kind.
> But we make his love too narrow by false limits of our own;
> And we magnify his strictness with a zeal he will not own.

This last need not be so. This little book shows that this only happens when, albeit from the most sincere motives, we separate religious belief from a right perception of our common humanity; when we insist on doctrine and moral codes of practice without being profoundly aware of pastoral questions. We see what happens when we elevate what must be, at best, approxi-

81. *The Church Hymnal, 5th Edition,* No 9.

mations into unbreakable codes of propriety that can never encompass the range and complexity of our human condition.

> If only men could,
> If only men would,
> Earth might be fair
> And all her peoples one.[82]

There is no magic divine wand that will cause all this to happen – we are not plants, or whales, or grubs under a master puppeteer. We are free beings, called into relationship with our Creator, and made in God's image. The Book of Jonah teaches us how God appeals to us within our freedom, reasoning with us, inviting us to consider things differently,

> Come now, and let us reason together, saith the Lord: though your sins be as scarlet, they shall be as white as snow; though they be red like crimson, they shall be as wool. *Isa 1:18*

and educating us by experience that may include the perplexing experience of his inaction.[83]

So the Book of Jonah shows us that the 'love of God is broader than the measure of man's mind'. It stands as a constant rebuke to our divisions, partitions, denominations and dissociations, and it rebukes with love, humour and patience – thus providing a model for our work of reconciliation and peace building.

It is a book for our times.

---

82. Clifford Bax: 'Turn back, O Man'. Quoted in *Jonah, Text, Exegesis and Exposition. The Interpreter's Bible.*

83. When Jesus refers to the book of Jonah in Matthew 12:38, he has perhaps been asked a similar question by Pharisees (Jonah types) looking for a miraculous sign of divinity. His response is, 'A wicked and adulterous generation asks for a miraculous sign! But none will be given to it except the sign of the prophet Jonah …' See whole passage Mt 12:38-45.

A note on the two faces of Jonah:
Jonah the individual remains painfully human throughout the narrative, yet more and more his predicament is seen to be iconic – even, in some sense Christ-like. The first picture (frontispiece) is a portrait of his human anguish; the second (above) his iconic significance for us all.

Select Bibliography

Berrigan, D., *A Book of Parables*, Seabury, New York, 1977

The Book of Common Prayer by Authority of the General Synod of the Church of Ireland. Columba Press, Dublin, 2004

Calvin, J., *Jonah, Micah and Nahum* in the *Geneva Series of Commentaries: The Minor Prophets, Volume 3,* Banner of Truth Trust, Edinburgh, 1986

Carlisle, T. J., *Journey with Jonah,* Forward Movement Publications, Ohio, 1984

Ceresko, A. R., Chapter 39 in *The New Jerome Biblical Commentary,* (eds. Brown, Fitzmyer and Murphy) Geoffrey Chapman, London, 1989

Church Hymnal, 5th Edition, OUP, Oxford, 2000

Ellul, J. (Tr. Bromiley, G. W.) *The Judgement of Jonah,* Eerdmans, Michigan 1971

Eliot, T. S., *The Four Quartets,* Faber and Faber, London, 1943

Girard, Rene, *The Scapegoat,* Johns Hopkins University Press, 1989

Harrison, G. B. (ed.), *A Book of English Poetry,* Penguin 1974

Horton, R. F. (ed.), *The Minor Prophets, The Century Bible,* Nelson and Sons, London

New Jerusalem Bible – text and some commentary, Darton, Longman and Todd, London 1984

Interpreter's Bible, A commentary in Twelve Volumes, Vol. 6, Abingdon, Nashville, 1980

Kendall, R. T., *Jonah An Exposition,* Biblical Classics Library, Paternoster Press 1978

Mc Gowan, Jean C., Chapter 39 of *The Jerome Biblical Commentary*, (eds. Brown, Fitzmyer, Murphy), Geoffrey Chapman, London, 1981

Melville, H., *Moby Dick*, Penguin Popular Classics, London, 1994

Murray, P., *A Journey with Jonah. The Spirituality of Bewilderment*, Columba Press, Dublin 2002

Pullman, Philip, *His Dark Materials*, Scholastic Children's Books, London, 2000

Sasson, Jack M., *Jonah A New Translation with Introduction, Commentary, and Interpretations by Jack M. Sasson,* Anchor Bible series, Doubleday, New York, 1990

Somerville, E. OE. and Ross, M., *The Real Charlotte*, North Books, 1998

Thompson, Francis, *The Hound of Heaven* in *Selected Poems*, Methuen, London, 1911

Torrance, T. F., *Theological Science*, Oxford University Press, Oxford, 1969

Torrance, T. F., *Divine and Contingent Order*, Oxford University Press, Oxford, 1981

Vanstone, W. H., *The Stature of Waiting*, Darton, Longman and Todd, London, 1982

Waugh, Evelyn, *A Handful of Dust*, Penguin Books, Harmondsworth, 1955